Learning to Teach Science

Learning to Teach Science:
Activities for Student Teachers and Mentors

Edited by
Martin Monk
and
Justin Dillon

The Falmer Press
(A member of the Taylor & Francis Group)
London • Washington, D.C.

UK   The Falmer Press, 4 John Street, London WC1N 2ET
USA   The Falmer Press, Taylor & Francis Inc., 1900 Frost Road, Suite 101, Bristol, PA 19007

First published in 1995

A catalogue record for this book is available from the British Library

Library of Congress Cataloging-in-Publication Data are available on request

ISBN 0 7507 0385 7 cased
ISBN 0 7507 0386 5 paper

Jacket design by Caroline Archer

Typeset in 10/12pt Bembo by
Graphicraft Typesetters Ltd., Hong Kong.

Printed in Great Britain by Burgess Science Press, Basingstoke on paper which has a specified pH value on final paper manufacture of not less than 7.5 and is therefore 'acid free'.

Contents

List of Figures and Tables

Preface

This book arises from the experiences of staff working over many years in training graduates for their entry into the teaching profession. It has always been axiomatic at King's College London that teachers in schools have an essential part to play in partnership with university staff in this training. Our work in developing school–college links has shown us that our co-tutors in schools find it hard to give the time and thought that they know is needed to develop their role to the full. They are well aware that far more is involved in preparing new teachers than putting them at the front of a class and criticizing their performance from the back.

My colleagues have started from the position that they can offer practical help for teachers in schools in our shared task of training. The ideas have been developed through years of experience from staff who themselves entered the university after several years as secondary teachers and who have renewed their contact by short periods of classroom teaching in schools in the last few years. I must acknowledge the many teachers in our partnership schools who have contributed to our course and from whom we have all learnt a great deal about the issues addressed in this book. We have been able to distil and fashion that experience into guidance that we believe will be helpful to teachers for whom their part in teacher training is only one of many important responsibilities which they carry out for their pupils and their schools.

In drawing up this material the authors have also had access to lessons learnt from research studies, in many of which they themselves have played a leading part. The advice on issues such as monitoring pupils' learning, or handling practical investigations with a set of thirty pupils, is based on research which has been carried out with teachers in their classrooms.

Reading through these chapters, I can see three main principles that underlie the approach adopted in them. The first is that, despite the variations in the spontaneous ability of new teachers, teaching is both an art and a craft that can be learned through hard work which demands close attention to numerous issues of detail.

The second is that the mode to which training should be aimed is that of the thoughtful and competent practitioner, one who can make effective use of a range of skills, who is well informed about the art and craft of teaching, who can reflect profitably on experience and whose first priority is care for the development of pupils.

The third, which subsumes the other two, is that all of us responsible for training, whether in schools or in universities, are committed to helping one another to offer high quality training which gives new entrants the best start possible to a career-long process of professional development. This book is one expression of my colleagues' commitment to that quality, and I recommend it to teachers in schools as a contribution to their share in that commitment.

Professor Paul Black
King's College London
July 1994

Introduction

Who is *Learning to Teach Science* for?

Mentors

The principal purpose of this book is to provide mentors with activities to be used with their student teachers. Reading this book should reassure teachers new to mentoring that this new role is not so difficult and that with practice and experience they can become highly effective.

Student Teachers

All fifty activities in the book are for student teachers. Therefore student teachers might usefully have their own copies so as to have direct access to the student teacher notes as well as the commentary for mentors. The notes for student teachers on their activities are always in a boxed format.

Science Teachers Generally

We think there is a lot of good advice in the activities. Experienced teachers will find it useful to have this text as an inventory against which to check their skills and knowledge. We would be disappointed if they did not find something new that they had not yet used or thought of.

Why read this book?

Learning Science

The activities for student teachers provide guidance on activities to help pupils learn science more effectively and more efficiently. We have built in advice on a wide range of different activities for pupils. Generally the third section of each chapter, (i.e. 3.3, 6.3, 8.3 etc.) is where we have placed the greatest variety of alternatives.

Introduction

Teaching

Better learning depends upon better teaching. Forty-five of the fifty activities focus on the classroom and the work of the teacher.

Mentorship

The mentor's brief, in each activity, provides background information and sets the scene. Each activity has an aim or objective to focus the activity for mentors and student teachers. Mentors can save time by directing student teachers to the students' notes. Chapter 1 is specifically written as general advice to mentors. Chapter 11 describes activities for reviewing student teachers' progress.

How is the book organized?

The activities are organized in two ways that run across each other, forming a matrix. There are chapters with activities sharing a common theme. There are phases of a student teacher's development which are identified by the place they have in the chapter and the numbering of the activity in the chapter.

Student Teachers' Development Reflected in the Activities through Chapters

- Early activities (i.e. 2.1, 3.1, 4.1 etc.) are for when student teachers have just arrived at the school and are finding their way about.
- Activities that follow are for when student teachers start team teaching lessons (i.e. 2.2, 3.2, 4.2 etc.).
- The third activity in each chapter is generally for when student teachers are teaching complete lessons (i.e. 2.3, 3.3, 4.3 etc.). This is where we have concentrated on introducing different activities for student teachers to trial and evaluate for incorporation into their own repertoires.
- The penultimate activities in each chapter (i.e. 2.4, 3.4, 4.4 etc.) are intended for use when student teachers have been teaching complete lessons for a few weeks. It is at this stage that they need to reflect on the implications of their planning, organizing and managing of activities for pupils. This is the time when student teachers might need some mid-point review (as in activity 11.4).
- The final activity of each chapter (i.e. 2.5, 3.5, 4.5 etc.) are intended for beyond the mid-point review and for when student teachers should be thinking in a broader way and looking forward to fuller professional control.

Chapters with Activities Grouped in Themes

The themes are:

- Observing teachers at work — which should be continued throughout the training of the student teacher and not just used at the initial stage.
- Activities for pupils — which forms the principal thrust of helping to direct the focus of work for the student teacher onto pupil activity.
- Planning and managing — which outlines the job specification for planning, organizing and managing activities for pupils.
- Investigations — which takes student teachers through one of the defining features of science.
- Communicating science — which alerts student teachers to a wide range of communication opportunities in science education.
- Science and knowledge — which introduces issues of the status and form of scientific knowledge.
- Science and people — which provides student teachers with pupil activities that can humanize science.
- Progression in pupils' ideas — which considers cognitive development and the possibilities of cognitive acceleration and differentiation.
- Assessment — which ranges from the routines of homework and marking through formative assessment to issues on summative assessment.

Chapter 1 and Chapter 11 bracket the whole enterprise. Chapter 1 opens with advice to mentors and Chapter 11 closes by providing mentors with activities for helping student teachers reflect on their professional progress and potential.

How Can the Book be Used?

Mentors

Mentors should read Chapter 1 first. This sets the scene for the job of mentoring. The three actions of team teaching, observing and debriefing are crucial to the job of the mentor. Good mentorship involves being skilled in these actions.

Scanning the first activities in each chapter (i.e. 2.1, 3.1, 4.1 etc.), mentors need to select activities for student teachers as it is unlikely that there will be time for all the activities. The activities selected need to be sequenced and linked so as to produce a scheme of work for the student teacher. The same process should be repeated when the student teacher starts team teaching (i.e. with activities 2.2, 3.2, 4.2 etc.). At the end of each phase of the student teacher's development, the appropriate activity from Chapter 11 should be carried out.

Introduction

Student Teachers

Student teachers need to read the notes in the boxes for the activities they are directed to by their mentors. They will learn more if they also read the Mentor's Brief for each activity. This should follow the reading of the activity and not precede it. Chapter 1 will initially be of little, or no interest, to student teachers.

Experienced Teachers

Activities at the end of each chapter may be most stimulating for experienced teachers. Having looked at the last activity in any one chapter, work backwards through the activities (i.e. 8.5, 8.4, 8.3, etc.) to find out why the last activity was there.

Heads of Department

Our advice is to read the book from cover to cover. Select chapters of interest and plan school-based INSET (in-service) around the activities in the chapter.

The Philosophy of the Activities

There are five principal ideas that underpin the whole of this book. Firstly, individuals are responsible for their own learning. Teachers and mentors can structure learning opportunities, but it is the pupil or student teacher who has to work at producing the change in themselves. This chimes with the current concerns of a constructivist view of learning. The constructivist philosophy of learning is most strongly expressed in Chapter 10, on progression in pupils' learning. In that chapter, the Piagetian theory of stages of knowledge making skills is described. Piagetian stage theory is also applied to the twin issues of progression and differentiation.

Secondly, a strong idea throughout the book is that to change one's cognitive practice requires a self-awareness. This is true both for pupils in changing their ideas about natural phenomena and for student teachers in changing their ideas about teaching and learning. This self-awareness can lead to closing the gap between where one is and where one wants to be. Activities for pupils focus on helping pupils to improve their knowledge and skills by thinking about their own learning of science. Activities for student teachers attempt to promote the reflective professional as a model.

A third idea that underpins the whole enterprise is that performance depends upon skills. Identification of skills is just one step in helping others to acquire those skills. This is true for the mentor helping the student teacher and for the teacher helping pupils. Personal and professional development is enhanced through sharpening our perceptions and conceptions of what constitutes a suitable repertoire of skills and how they might be learnt.

Fourthly, the idea of cooperation and mutual help is important to the activity of both learning science and learning to teach science. We advocate a team-teaching approach from the start. We feel that observation is a continuing activity that improves the professional practice of mentor and student teacher alike. We think that pupils should be encouraged to work cooperatively in their learning of science.

Fifthly, certainly not lastly, but perhaps fundamentally, the book is written with the idea that we can change. Education is possible. One would think that this should go without saying. And yet, the culture of the school can be such that this idea is sometimes forgotten, and even worse, suppressed. As mentor, student teacher, teacher, INSET organiser, pupil, we have to believe that we can, and will, do better.

The source of the activities and ideas

Most of the activities in this book derive from the routine work of science teacher trainers at King's College London in the training of science teachers. Tutors at King's have both long and wide experience in such training activities. The Nuffield Science projects of the late 1960s and 1970s were based at Chelsea College, before it joined with the education faculty of King's College London. Tutors at King's act as consultants to science education projects around the world. Research into science education continues to be a flourishing part of the work of tutors at King's. That breadth and depth of experience is reflected in the wide range of focused activities for student teachers contained in this book.

Science Teacher Mentoring

Introduction

This chapter focuses on the role of the mentor and science teacher development. It addresses two fundamental questions: what is involved in becoming a science teacher and what does being a mentor to student science teachers involve? It has been written specifically for science teachers (the mentors) but it may also be useful for teachers responsible for student teachers in a whole-school context. The chapter begins with a section on teacher development. This is followed by a section on the role of the mentor in which three key actions of mentoring are discussed: team teaching, observing and debriefing. A third section looks at issues which are specific to the training of teachers of science. The fourth section looks at issues related to working with mature students.

In the UK, as part of the wholesale changes which took place in primary and secondary education in the 1980s and 1990s, teacher training was systematized and regulated more rigorously than had previously been the case. Although teacher training institutions still have control over the detailed content of courses, they are subject to government regulation. In 1992, the Department for Education (DFE), acting on advice from CATE (the Council for the Accreditation of Teacher Education), gave guidance about the nature of initial teacher education. It was explicitly stated that 'the planning and management of training courses should be the shared responsibility of higher education institutions and schools in partnership'.

Many training institutions already had well-established links with local schools, often maintained through ex-students who had been appointed to jobs in the area when they qualified. There were a variety of approaches used to structure teacher training courses but they all relied on some element of teaching practice ('placement' or 'practicum'). With the implementation of the 1993 Education Act, the commonality between the courses offered has increased and the links between schools and training institutions have became formalized as 'partnerships'. Even the name by which teachers responsible for students has changed from co-tutor, school tutor or supervisor to 'mentor'.

According to the Department for Education: 'Students should be given opportunities to observe good teachers at work in . . . classrooms, to participate with experienced practitioners in teaching their specialist subjects and, as confidence develops, to undertake periods of continuous whole class teach ing.' The mentor's role predominantly involves making sure that student teachers *observe, participate* and *teach* and, at the same time, *develop* their confidence. All this is in the context of both the whole-school approach to the student teachers' progress (which may not be the responsibility of the science department) and the college-based aspects of the course which you should be aware of through links with the college.

Section 1   Teacher Development

How do teachers develop, not just during their training, but throughout their careers? Is it a process of copying the style and skills of other teachers? Do teachers change to fit the demands of teaching and does teaching itself change as society evolves? Student teachers begin their teaching practice with many years of experience of being taught both at school and at university or college. They will have seen teachers represented on television and read about them in newspapers. They will generally be able to identify what they think a good teacher does, at least from their point of view usually as a successful student. These images and ideas are well-established and resistant to change. This is not necessarily a bad thing and at least offers models that the student teachers can use to compare with their own experience. On the other hand, the picture may well be naive and one-dimensional. Few students, even those with teacher parents, understand the stress and strain or the joys of teaching in today's schools. Part of learning to teach involves the student teacher examining his or her own views of teachers and of teaching.

Humans are good at copying: it often feels more comfortable to copy than it does to think things through for yourself especially if you are a beginner. Good student teachers are able to go beyond copying and to discover their own potentials and to put into practice their own philosophies. This requires not only ability and motivation but also freedom and support. What is critical for student teachers (and for practising teachers) is the skill of reflecting on what they see and do.

On Reflection

A theme that runs both implicitly and explicitly throughout this book is that of teachers as reflective practitioners. That is to say, the model of teacher development that we espouse stands or falls on the ability of student teachers to evolve as teachers in the light of their understanding of what they have experienced. Figure 1.1 below shows a simplified learning cycle for the training process. The process is represented as being sequential and without end. Experience is followed by reflection which is focused, through discussion, onto future plans.

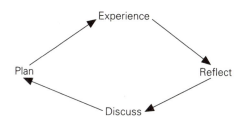

Figure 1.1: A simplified learning cycle

The assumption that we make is that people are able to change what they do as practitioners and that they are able to develop the skill to evaluate their own performance, with the help of other information and other people. Another assumption that we make is that people are willing to change what they do in the light of evidence that suggests that change may be desirable. This is more problematic and is one of the stumbling blocks on the road to maximum development of potential. It is in this area that the job of the mentor finds its biggest challenges.

Competence-based Training

One approach to teacher development emphasizes the idea of professional competence. In defining what should constitute the curriculum of a teacher training course, the Department for Education states that:

> Higher education institutions, schools and students should focus on the competences of teaching throughout the whole period of initial training. The progressive development of these competences should be monitored regularly during initial training. Their attainment at a level appropriate to newly qualified teachers should be the objective of every student taking a course of initial training.

The competences (issued as an Appendix to DFE Circular 9/92) which should be progressively developed and which are expected of newly qualified teachers are grouped under the following headings:

- Subject Knowledge
- Subject Application
- Class Management
- Assessment and Recording of Pupils' Progress
- Further Professional Development

The competences themselves are given in Appendix 1 (pp 208–211) and are referred to later in this chapter.

Teachers experienced with competence-based training will be aware that there are problems with the implied model of assessment. How, for example, is the ability to 'maintain pupils' interest and motivation' assessed adequately, accurately and fairly. Can any teacher say confidently that they have this competence, whatever the school, whatever the class, whatever the topic, whatever the time of year or even the weather?

The competences should be regarded as targets for the development of teaching skills within a broader and richer picture of becoming a professional teacher. As teachers, pupils and parents know, a teacher's attitudes may well be at least as important as a teacher's level of skill. At a simplistic level, the mentor can use competences as a guide for helping student teachers to develop their knowledge, skills and attitudes for the benefit of the pupils they teach.

Teacher Knowledge and Skills

Developing as a science teacher invariably involves making many changes in terms of personal knowledge. Lee Shulman (1987) attempted to classify teacher knowledge into seven areas:

- Specialist subject teaching knowledge (how to teach the subject)
- Knowledge of classroom management and organization
- Knowledge of the curriculum (including the national curriculum, examination syllabuses and departmental schemes of work)
- Content knowledge (i.e. knowledge about their subject)
- Knowledge of pupils and of how they may learn
- Knowledge of the context of education (including cultural and societal issues, gender issues, school management, etc.)
- Knowledge of education's ends, purposes and values, and of its philosophical and historical grounds.

In general, you should expect to focus on the first three areas throughout most of the student teachers' teaching practice and underpin their progress through developing their knowledge of the last three. That leaves 'Content knowledge': generally one hopes that student teachers' knowledge of science, in particular, of their own specialist subject would be adequate for the purposes of teaching up to and including A-level. In the real world things are different. Many teachers realize that only through teaching do you develop a clear understanding of a subject (as opposed to a knowledge of 'the facts'). Under pressure in the classroom, student teachers may be driven to invent a science, that is unknown outside of the walls of their laboratory, in order to maintain continuity and flow in classroom action. Unfortunately this wrong information will disappear into pupils' books to be recalled later. Careful preparation by the student teacher can reduce this risk. Regular checking of the student teacher's plans is critically important for mentors.

Christine Cunningham and William Carlsen of Cornell University have recently amended Shulman's list to include 'Knowledge of the sociology of science', which reflects the moves during the 1980s and 1990s to include the nature of science in the curriculum. This is touched on later in this chapter and is the focus of Chapters 7 and 8.

Section 2   The Role of the Mentor

Implicit in the use of the word 'mentor' is a view of the relationship between the teacher concerned and the student teacher. Do you see yourself as a trainer, a tutor or an educator? Whichever model you have, it may not be the same as the model in the head of the student teacher who may see you either as the fount of knowledge to be drunk dry as soon as possible or a model of perfection to be copied in every detail.

The roles of a mentor are many and varied and at any one time you may be any of the following:

- Adviser (e.g. suggesting how to handle 'difficult' pupils)
- Assessor (e.g. deciding whether the student teacher has passed or failed)
- Counsellor (e.g. helping to alleviate the stress and strain)
- Guide (e.g. emphasizing the consequences of particular strategies)
- Intermediary (e.g. sorting out mistakes that have been made)
- Observer (e.g. of lessons)
- Motivator (e.g. when the student teacher is wondering whether to continue)
- Role model (e.g. as a teacher and as a 'professional').

Even more importantly it is to be hoped that you become a trusted and respected friend. For many student teachers, teaching practice is one of the most challenging experiences that they will ever face. Standing in front of thirty or more adolescents who you think may be bored, teaching something that you don't know thoroughly, taxes even the most experienced teacher. Student teachers are more likely to listen to and act upon advice from people they see as friends than those they feel are enemies.

What Makes a Good Mentor?

Mentoring itself is problematic, partly because it involves so many roles and responsibilities and partly because of the possible conflicts of the needs of the school, the pupils and other staff. The training that mentors receive varies considerably from school to school. A survey by Anne Williams (1993) found that the majority of mentors, in her sample, felt competent to do these jobs:

- organizing a student teacher's timetable;
- helping a student teacher with resources;
- helping student teachers to meet other staff;
- discussing lesson preparation;
- helping with teaching strategies;
- helping with classroom management;
- discussing preparation before a lesson;
- observing a lesson;
- discussing a lesson after observing it.

About half the mentors felt that they needed training in the following actions:

- helping the student teacher to set targets;
- counselling student teachers;
- providing written feedback on an observed lesson;
- assessing student teachers' whole performance;
- helping with university assignments.

This may indicate that the teachers see the tutoring and counselling role as being more problematic or it may be that they are simply reflecting that they have had less training and experience of those areas of being a mentor. The rest of this chapter focuses on the first four of the areas where teachers have expressed the desire for more training.

One of the biggest dilemmas of being a mentor is working with a student teacher who is clearly having problems. Failing someone who you have been responsible for and have got to know and like is difficult, unsatisfactory and often stressful. It is less unsatisfactory if you have:

- agreed clear and reasonable objectives;
- monitored progress and given accurate feedback;
- made the process of learning to teach stepwise, gradual and stimulating;
- provided useful advice and adequate support.

It is less stressful if the student teacher realizes that he or she has got problems and appreciates that you are doing all that you can to help. Somebody somewhere was responsible for passing the small but significant number of teachers who are unfair to pupils, who do not plan adequately, who do not know their subject and who do not care.

Student teachers report that good mentors offer useful advice, provide consistent and useful written and spoken comments, devote adequate time, liaise effectively with college tutors, guide without prescription and allow the opportunity to experiment within reason.

Being a mentor involves balancing the needs of the student, the school, the pupils and yourself. Sometimes these needs pull you in different directions and there is never enough time to do everything well. Your student teacher may not, initially at least, be aware of, or be sensitive to the needs of the school, the pupils or you. Basically, a good mentor is someone who creates a situation in which a student teacher's potential is developed to the maximum and who is able to relate the end performance to the standards required of a newly-qualified teacher (NQT).

Many experienced mentors will have their own strategies and styles. However, the job of mentoring is changing and becoming more formalized and may even be contractually based. Teachers will need to look critically at their own practice if they are to ensure that they have adapted to the new challenges. The rest of this chapter focuses primarily on possible strategies that mentors can adopt. Teachers new to mentoring may need to consider the strategies more thoroughly than more experienced teachers.

Action 1   Team-teaching

For many student teachers, the time when their confidence grows and when they feel 'proper' teachers is when they are alone in the room. However, it is better for them to be itching to get started than to start them too soon — generally. Part of the problem is that the transition from observing to teaching often occurs before the student teacher is really mentally prepared. Indeed the notion of going solo may lead to a false dichotomy in the student teacher's mind — doing it with help and doing it alone. It is better to think of a continual spectrum, with observing at one end and teaching complete lessons unaided at the other.

Team teaching is not something that is part of a teacher's everyday experience — there just aren't enough teachers to practice it. However, the advantages that it offers in terms of managing a class, being able to spread the load and keep up the pace of a lesson are tremendous. With practice and a good blend of personalities and styles it can be almost instinctive and seamless but it does require planning and patience.

It is usually better to start the student teacher working with younger pupils in well-behaved classes and, if you have them, with post-16 groups. Introduce the student teacher by name and explain that he or she is another teacher (introducing someone as 'a student' may not be particularly helpful nor as accurate as 'a teacher'). It may be better if the student teacher is standing next to you when he or she is introduced and not sitting at the back. Pupils will pick up clues from the way that you interact with the student teacher: if you treat the student teacher as your equal, you will be setting the example for the class.

Allocate groups of pupils or specific tasks to the student teacher. Tasks include: going round during a lesson checking that people are working safely; checking to see if pupils have done the homework set last lesson; asking each group if they can explain the aim of the experiment they are working on. The purpose of these activities is to get the student teacher to practice talking with pupils, moving around the class (while watching everybody else) and thinking on his or her feet. Pupils will benefit by having someone else to help them and you will also benefit by having another person to share the load. Engaging the student teacher in the management of groups is also to be encouraged: 'Can you go round and check that all the class is wearing their safety glasses please Mr. Jones?', shares your authority and shows the class that the student teacher has authority too. At the end of the activity you should talk to each other and to the class: 'I thought Chris's results were particularly excellent, didn't you Ms. Brown?' By bringing the student teacher into immediate, non-threatening contact in a way that he or she can be positive about the class is a more natural process.

As time goes by, the student teacher should begin to teach parts of lessons. Splitting the lesson into chunks allows you and the student teacher to take it in turns as well as serving to make the structure of the lesson more explicit. The student teacher can start lessons, do demonstrations, introduce a video or collect ideas from groups while you write them on the board.

Action 2   Observing

Having someone watching you can be stressful, it can affect the pupils and it can also be uncomfortable to the observer. So why do we do it? Judging from student teachers' comments, it is not something that many mentors do regularly nor do in a systematized way. Student teachers often report that the feedback that they receive is perfunctory, often spoken not written and sometimes inconsistent. This section looks at the process of observation and presents some suggestions to improve the quality and the effectiveness of observation.

The word 'observation' itself indicates that the act of watching is, or has been, regarded as the critical process. Observation of a student teacher's lesson is not in itself formative. The formative nature of the process depends not only on the data collected but also on the accuracy of the interpretation and on the follow-up action taken. At a simple level there are three steps that need to be considered:

- *Step 1* Before a lesson — discussing plans
- *Step 2* During the lesson — observing and recording data
- *Step 3* After the lesson — discussing the data.

Most of the comments below apply particularly to the first few occasions you are watching the student teacher taking his or her first complete lessons. They can, however, be adapted to any lesson. Because the debriefing is so important, it is treated separately.

Before the lesson

There is a difference between discussing lesson planning and discussing what it is that you are looking for prior to observing teaching. In the former, you are helping by suggesting methods and resources: in the latter you are finding out what is going to happen and where it will take place. The student teacher should know what you are looking for and how you are going to record your data. He or she should be able to suggest aspects of the teaching that he or she wants you to focus on.

Decide where you are going to sit so that you can see without being too obtrusive. Tempting as it is to sit in an adjoining room you will not be able to see as much as if you are in the classroom or laboratory. Decide which method of recording data you are going to use. You should have a copy of the lesson plan and either an observation schedule or a blank piece of paper (or both).

Agree a system of communication between yourselves: suggest that the student teacher comes and sits next to you during the lesson or that you go and see them when you need to say something. Comments can be more influential when made during a lesson than after it. The skill is in making appropriate comments in a positive manner: 'Keep an eye on John, he's not written much'; 'I liked the explanation of the experiment — don't forget to tell them when they've got five minutes left'; or 'They seem to be getting on fine, though I think Sarah's group need some help with the graph'.

During the lesson

With practice, the student teacher will become used to your presence. However, at the beginning she may either avoid eye-contact with you (and probably ignore pupils in the area of the room where you are sitting) or they will be watching you for clues and interpreting what you do. Try not to give signals that the student teacher could interpret as personal criticism unless you have to. It is better that you say and do nothing when mistakes are made or when opportunities are lost *unless* it affects the safety of the class or of the student teacher. However, nodding with approval or smiling at jokes can be supportive and well-received.

Think what you're going to say to the student teacher during the lesson — can you give them some positive feedback together with a helpful suggestion or question. Make sure that when you talk to the student teacher that you can both see *all* the pupils, don't face each other as it limits your view.

Towards the end of the lesson, think about what you are going to say. You should jot down a few key comments based on the points that you were looking at and maybe one or two other points that you want to comment on. You need to be able to find evidence in your notes to support the points that you are going to make.

Action 3   Debriefing

Post-lesson debriefing is the time when your skills as counsellor, guide, motivator and adviser will be most severely tested. Bringing an over-confident student teacher back to earth needs as much tact as raising the spirits of a depressed over-critical student.

Your *priorities* are:

- to elicit the student teacher's observations and feelings carefully;
- to help the student teacher to analyse what happened and why it happened;
- to give accurate and relevant observations of what you observed;
- to assist the student teacher to think about how he or she could improve on what has just been taught;
- to guide the student teacher to suggest strategies for improving the performance next time he or she teaches;
- to set the student teacher's performance in context with his or her overall development.

Debriefing is best done in private in the same room as the lesson took place. If that is possible, sit somewhere that allows the technicians to clear away without feeling that they are in the way. If it is not possible then you must agree a time and a place to meet, though you should make some immediate comment so that the student teacher is not left wondering what you thought.

In debriefing it is important that you can maintain eye-contact with the student teacher without being face-to-face. Sitting at ninety degrees to each other is a good strategy. Having a table to put your notes on so that you both can see them is important too.

Generally it is better to ask questions with the aim of encouraging the student teacher to reflect on his or her performance than it is to start by telling the student teacher what you observed. Questions to ask will include the following:

- What did you think was good about that lesson?
- How could you improve upon what you did?
- What would you do differently? Why?
- What would you do the same? Why?
- What were your main objectives?
- How successful were you in achieving those objectives? How do you know?
- What assumptions did you make? Were they justified?
- Why did you do X? Did it work?

During this phase you are trying to find out how accurate the student teacher is in gauging the effectiveness of his or her lessons and also setting an agenda for self-evaluation, later. These are the questions that you want the student teacher to be asking him or herself after each lesson.

Start your feedback by making positive remarks about his/her efforts or attainment (or both if appropriate). Go through the three or four main points that you want to make and give your opinion and your evidence. Does the student teacher agree with your comments? For each point, you must make a positive suggestion for improvement. Offer whatever help is necessary in terms of time or resources.

Debriefing is successful when the student teacher receives an accurate evaluation in such a way that she is motivated to keep on doing what she does well and change where necessary. She must see what should be changed, how she could go about implementing the change and what to expect when she is successful. For example, she may realize that she did not communicate the method for an experiment successfully. You may suggest (or better still, she may suggest) asking pupils to explain what they have to do before starting the experiment. She would expect that the pupils would give an accurate description of what to do, where to get the apparatus and of what the aim of the experiment was.

This is a critical time to focus on changing the student teacher's performance. You may wish to write down what the student teacher agrees to do differently next time and to remind them of this before the next lesson. The other teachers in the department need to know this information too. You may need to photocopy your notes for those of your colleagues whose lesson the student teacher is teaching so as to minimize the chance that the student teacher is given conflicting advice.

Section 3   Specific Issues Related to Science Teaching

Science teachers have a broad range of responsibilities in any school. They use potentially dangerous chemicals and apparatus, work with pupils in rivers and ponds, and serve as a source of information on topics ranging from AIDS to acid rain. This section focuses on some of these facets of science teaching and suggests ways in which student teachers can learn about them.

Safety

One of the major areas of concern to science teachers is safety. School laboratories are safer than school lavatories because science teachers and technicians have adopted a culture of safe working that sometimes goes to extremes. However, safety is the one aspect of science teaching that a student teacher cannot afford to get wrong at the beginning. One of the major responsibilities of the mentor is to check that the student:

- knows the risks of what they are planning to do;
- knows how to deal with spills, burns and cuts;
- knows where to turn off the gas and electricity;

- knows where the fire extinguishers, fire blankets and first-aid kits are located;
- knows what to say to make sure that pupils are aware of safety procedures.

Safety glasses are a major concern of student teachers. During observation they may see that pupils do not wear safety glasses and that teachers are not rigorous in enforcing the departmental safety policy. This is something that should be discussed with the student teacher. The safety practices that are adopted at the start of a career may be the ones that are continued. It is your responsibility to make sure that the student teacher acts safely and to make sure that the pupils work safely too.

Sex Education

Possibly because teaching practice often coincides with frogs spawning and bulbs bursting into bloom, student teachers often find themselves teaching 'reproduction'. Some schools adopt a policy of not giving students any classes sex education involving. If you decide that the student teacher should teach elements of sex education they must be briefed on the legal implications and school policy. This is essential. As well as accurate information, student teachers need to have strategies to deal with 'awkward questions' in advance of lessons.

Fieldwork

Science contributes significantly to environmental education in different ways. As well as teaching about the environment and environmental issues, science teachers often use the environment as a stimulus for teaching and as a resource through fieldwork in and out of school. Although teaching practice placements may not coincide with any fieldwork students should be made aware of the opportunities and the responsibilities that are involved.

Health Education

Another responsibility of science teachers that is not necessarily shared with other subject teachers is that of health education. Science teachers may well have a more thorough knowledge of health-related issues than other staff and the science department may take a major role in the school's overall health education policy and practice. Student teachers need to be made aware of the school policy (if any exists). They should spend some time during their school experience studying the role that science teachers play in the overall delivery of health education throughout the school.

Section 4 Mature Students

Although all students are mature, some are more mature than others. The variation can be extraordinary. Some students, particularly on part-time courses, may have combinations of families, mortgages, part-time jobs, child-care needs, and so on. They may have very high qualifications, experience in industry (possibly at a senior level), experience as a school governor or be working as an instructor in another school (Circular 9/92 requires student teachers to train in two schools). Many of these attributes enable them to make positive contributions during their training. Often, they look more like 'proper teachers' in pupils' eyes than the average student teacher or, even, the average newly-qualified teacher. They may have well-established views about schools and teaching, gained through being parents. They may have had years of experience of dealing with obstinate and rude children — their own! Some of these views may be difficult to change and may make your job more difficult. They may be undertaking a major change in their lives, sometimes not entirely of their own choosing. Working with such experienced student teachers offers its own challenges but it can also offer remarkable rewards. The important thing is to draw a sharp distinction between their experiences as parents, scientists, or whatever, and their experience in teaching.

Chapter 2

Observing Science Teachers at Work

Aim

Observing teachers in action is important not only at the start of training but also as the student teacher progresses and develops skills. It is essential that observation sessions are structured, focusing on a specific aspect, so that the student teacher can tease out the elements that make up a lesson and modify and adapt what has been witnessed to suit a personal teaching style. Even when the student teacher has advanced to teaching whole lessons, it is still important to continue observing lessons. Early observations will provide student teachers with repertoires from which they can choose when linking activities together in their own lesson plans. Later observations will allow student teachers to refine their developing skills by focusing on details that were previously unnoticed. The aims of this chapter are therefore to help student teachers to:

- structure their observations in a systematic manner;
- focus their attention on specific aspects of classroom action;
- reflect on how their own teaching may be changed;
- observe how the choice of activities for pupils realizes curricular aims.

Introduction

Observation is an important process in science. Philosophers of science will quickly point out that no observation is theory free. Science teachers know this from their work with pupils. What is true of pupils looking down a microscope, at a test-tube or at an electric circuit is equally true for student teachers watching science classes. What you perceive depends upon your concepts. Young children, given the role of parent or teacher in a play, act as a rather bossy person: their experience is of people telling them what to do. This also tends to be their perception of a teacher's job. Recent university graduates, on the other hand, tend to see teaching as transmitting information. This reflects their recent experiences of learning. Neither young children nor graduates conceive of teaching as the management of learning experiences. To see teaching as management you need help in focusing in on the way teachers act as managers.

Activity 2.1a focuses the student teacher's attention on systematic observation, a key feature of science itself. Observations of teachers can be repeated with different teachers in different subject areas and comparisons made of different teaching styles. A straightforward observation schedule is used with recordings made every three minutes. Profiles of teachers can be built up in terms of their own personal styles. Profiles across subjects might also be compared if time allows. Activity 2.1b then considers triads of teachers who are compared so that similarities and differences can be used to highlight the actions teachers take in managing their classes.

Activity 2.2 is intended for use when student teachers have started on team-teaching parts of lessons under the supervision of yourself, as mentor, and your colleagues. Student teachers will be managing small pieces of action, so they need to carefully observe how other teachers act. They need consciously to reflect upon how they themselves are acting. This is a critical period for student teachers and you will find yourself spending a good deal of time discussing their preparation and their performance. Reference to Chapter 1 on how to work with student teachers is vital to your success as a mentor. Your own skills can be improved if you reflexively consider how you are helping the student teacher: a learning period for all concerned.

A third form of observation is introduced in activity 2.3. This coincides with student teachers taking responsibility for complete lessons. Student teachers need to cope with lessons from start to finish and so a more open-ended approach to recording their observations follows. The key element is on noting times for activities. It is intended that this should help focus student teachers' attention on the need to plan pupil activity and this should build on the work on writing objectives in section 3.2 and lesson planning in section 4.1a. You may need to make these links for the student teacher and refer to this previous work.

Teachers interact with individual pupils across the room when they elicit pupils' ideas, give instructions and generally manage the activities of the pupils. In activity 2.3b attention is turned to which individuals the teacher interacts with. The intention is to log, and then analyse those interactions for patterns. This is relevant to activity 6.2b on 'sharing ideas' and could be used as follow-up observation.

In activity 2.4b attention is turned to the pupils. It is well worth spending time observing how pupils who have achieved different classroom reputations spend their time. Experienced teachers think they know tacitly how different pupils behave. But rarely do they have the luxury of engaging in systematic observation. Student teachers have an opportunity here that will be denied them in the future when under the pressure of a full workload. What are the differences between the classroom lives of higher and lower achievers? As professionals, teachers have a responsibility for adjusting the tasks and demands they make on pupils so that the pupils' learning is maximized. From their observations student teachers are invited to consider how this might be done.

When student teachers are preparing to review and revise schemes of work they need to return to the classroom to observe with a new perspective. In activity 2.5 the observations take on a more holistic viewpoint. The focus is upon how aims are realized in lessons. Student teachers are invited to take a critical stance as they themselves are invited to prepare alternative activities for their schemes of work. In keeping with the more holistic viewpoint the recording is in terms of the prose of a written report.

2.1a   Observation Schedule

Mentor's Brief

Objectives   • Student teachers should be able to make systematic observations of teachers at work.
  • Student teachers should be able to conduct a conversation about lessons focusing on the nature and variation in teachers' actions.

Timing   • 6 or 7 lessons for the student teacher
  • 20 minutes twice a week for discussion with the mentor

Background

There are many different observation schedules available of varying levels of sophistication. One of the easiest to use is that which requires the observer to note down, for pre-determined intervals, what is happening at that exact moment. (See Figure 2.1.) Such schedules are essentially sampling instruments, the time interval between sample observations corresponding to the size of mesh in a net. All schedules compromise between detail and workability. A three minute time interval captures detail at about the right level for a student teacher and is within the skills of a novice observer.

Instructions

  • Consult the departmental timetable to select a range of different classes with different colleagues for the student teacher to observe.
  • Provide your student teacher with a timetable for observations.
  • Provide your student teacher with multiple copies of the observation schedule overleaf.
  • Talk through the observation schedule, and its use, with the student teacher. The columns of boxes are for what is happening at the stroke of a three minute interval. One only ticks for actions taking place at that very moment. The observer makes a mark in the appropriate box. Generally there will be both pupil and teacher action marks.

School ——————————— Date ——————————— Class ——————————— Start time ———————
Teacher ——————————— Topic ———————

		3	6	9	12 etc.																				Total
TEACHER	organizing by talking																								
	demonstrating with apparatus																								
	discussing																								
	writing for copying																								
	trouble shooting pupils' experiments																								
	other																								
PUPILS	listening to teacher																								
	copying from board																								
	working from text worksheet																								
	experimenting																								
	other																								

Observer ———————

Figure 2.1: Observation schedule with predetermined intervals

Coming in and going out will involve the 'other' category for pupils, as may other pupil actions.

- A tally is made at the extreme right-hand box to give a lesson/teacher profile.
- Discuss the student teacher's observations.

Discussion points

The tally in the right-hand column will provide a profile that is appropriate to that size of time interval. Classrooms can be busy places and student teachers need to judge the overall pupil activity. The combination of observation of both teacher and pupil actions allows for the recording of the actions of skilled teachers who have good classroom control and who discuss or organize only when the pupils are listening. Similarly, teachers who trouble-shoot by circulating amongst pupil groups when they are experimenting can be picked out from the recorded observations. Student teachers should be encouraged to discuss any other patterns they notice in what they judge to be successful and less successful lessons. It is instructive to compare lesson profiles for the same teacher as well as profiles between teachers.

2.1b Comparing Actions using Triads

Mentor's Brief

Objective • Student teachers should be able to state a set of behaviours for effective classroom action which they can use to guide their own actions.

Time • 1 hour for the student teacher working alone
• $\frac{1}{2}$ hour for discussion with the mentor

Background

This technique, of presenting three examples and asking for the respondent to explain how two are similar and yet different to the third, is derived from a standard social psychology procedure. George Kelly (1955) is credited with being its originator.

Instructions

- Direct the student teacher to the activity.
- Discuss the list of actions with the student teacher.

2.1b Comparing Actions using Triads

Student Teacher's Brief

Objective

You should be able to articulate a set of teachers' behaviour which you can use to guide your own classroom actions.

Instructions

You should attempt this only after a week or two of observation. The activity is best carried out in a room in which you are will be undisturbed.

- Write out on separate cards the names of each of the teachers that you have observed.
- Order the cards across the table.
- Select the first three in the line. Move them to a position in front you.
- Decide on a pair that share a common behaviour in the classroom that is not shared by the third teacher.
- Write down the action and its opposite.
- Systematically work through all the cards presenting triads to yourself.
- Record the nominated action and its opposite in each case.

Constructs like, 'Keeps control' versus 'Doesn't keep control' are far too global to be useful in helping you change your repertoire of managerial actions. However constructs like 'Has everything to hand' versus 'Doesn't know where things are' are more useful. If you are aware of these differences you are on the way to acting appropriately yourself. The more concrete the constructs and their opposites the more achievable they are in terms of your actions.

2.2 Observation with Higher Resolution

Mentor's Brief

Objective • Student teachers should be able to use their observations of other teachers at work to improve their own contributions to team teaching parts of lessons.

Time • 6 or 7 lessons for the student teacher
• $\frac{1}{2}$ hour at the end of school, twice a week, for the mentor

Background

This activity should be carried out in conjunction with activity 4.2. It is important that student teachers continue with their observations when they start to team-teach alongside yourself and your colleagues. Some of this observation can be within the same lesson they are team-teaching. If this is the case, the student teachers need time to write up their notes after their observation.

Instructions

- Discuss a schedule of continuing observation with the student teacher.
- When the student teacher is running their part of the lesson, either you or your colleagues should keep notes on the student teacher's actions. This should be done as part of activity 4.2.

  These notes will be useful for providing the student teacher with feedback. As with the student teacher, the focus of your attention should be on his or her observable behaviour. They can change their actions if their behaviour is brought to their attention. Student teachers often prefer written feedback as they can consider the comments at their leisure.
- Meet with the student teacher to discuss the written reports on each of the specific activities that have been focused on.

Discussion points

Adopting the right level of detail in observing extended action requires careful consideration. Student teachers may focus in on very small details that, by and large, miss the structure and pattern of the whole action. You will need to guide their observations where you feel they are missing the point or nit-picking at details. It might be useful to use a Chinese-box metaphor within which the activity contains actions, which contain smaller acts. The student teacher's briefing directs them to write out a chronological sequence of teacher-acts from the observations. You will need to inspect this record to check the level of detail they are focusing on.

2.2 Observation with Higher Resolution

Student Teacher's Brief

The intention here is that you should increase the level of detail you focus on in your observations. What are the specific teacher actions that produce successful demonstrations, explanations, eliciting of pupils' ideas, working from texts books, comprehension activities, practical work, investigations, and so on?

This phase of observation should coincide with you starting to team-teach alongside your mentor and colleagues. It will therefore be appropriate to use your observations of others to help you to think more critically about your own actions. There is a learning cycle that you should be consciously aware of.

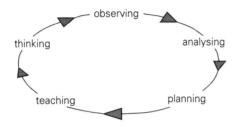

Figure 2.2: A learning cycle

Objective

You should be able to use your observations of other teachers at work to improve your own contributions to team-teaching parts of lessons.

Instructions

- What will be the principal activity for the lesson you are to observe?
  Plan your observations in conjunction with activity 4.2.
- Go into the lesson and take part, as a helper/auxiliary teacher until the teacher starts on the activity that is the focus of your attention.
- Note down the actions the teacher takes as he or she goes through the activity in a chronological sequence.
- When the activity is finished, take a fresh sheet of paper and write out an orderly sequence for the teacher's actions. Add a commentary.
  Don't take any further part in the lesson until you have finished this work.
- You may wish to share your observations with the teacher after the lesson, if there is time. Do remember that science teachers are very busy and need to have all their wits about them as they go from class to class. It may be better to defer conversation until the end of the school day. Even then, ask if this will be possible.
- When you have built up a collection of observations on a similar activity write a report for discussion with your mentor.
  You may have a number of reports to write up. For instance on:

pencil and paper tasks
demonstrations with question and answer routines
class practicals
explanations at the board with question and answer routines.

- Discuss your report for each pupil activity with your mentor.

2.3a Complete Lessons

Mentor's Brief

Objective • Student teachers should be able to improve their lesson planning as they take into account the constraints of time.

Time • 6 or 7 lessons for the student teacher
- $\frac{1}{2}$ hour at the end of school, twice a week, for the mentor

Background .

Observation should now focus on the way in which complete lessons are structured. Time is a very important constraint on lessons and needs careful attention in lesson planning. Student teachers should have been introduced to lesson plans with activity 4.1. The observation technique to be used in this activity is one that parallels the lesson plan used for illustration in activity 4.1.

Instructions

- You should arrange to formally meet with the student teacher at least twice a week.
- You may wish to look at a student teacher's lesson plans at the same time that you discuss his or her observation records.

2.3a Complete Lessons

Student Teacher's Brief

This third observation activity is to be used in conjunction with your work on lesson planning and teaching complete lessons in activity 4.3. Once again you should keep in mind the cycle of observing, analysing, planning, teaching, thinking.

Objective

You should be able to improve your planning as you take into account the constraints of time.

Instructions

- Refer to the lesson plan in activity 4.1.
  You will be using a similar format for your observations.
- You will need a watch or small clock to keep track of the time.
- In recording your observations of lessons watch for changes of activity or action on the part of the teacher.
- On the left-hand side of your record write down the time at which things happen.
- Record the actions alongside the times.
- Compare your lesson plans with the observations you record.
- Look for patterns in your observations.
- Discuss your observations and lesson plans with your mentor.

2.3b Interactions with Pupils

Mentor's Brief

Objective • Student teachers should improve the distribution of their interactions with pupils as they become more aware of the interaction patterns of themselves and others.

Time • 6 or 7 lessons for the student teacher
• $\frac{1}{2}$ hour at the end of school, twice a week, for the mentor

Instructions

This observation activity continues the work started in activity 6.2b and can be used to sharpen up the points made there through the collection of observation data.

- Briefly discuss the task with the student teacher.
- Use some of your observation time to carry out a reciprocal exercise on the student teacher's lessons.
- Discuss the student teacher's observations of other teachers and your observations of the student teacher's current practice.

A variation on this activity is to record the time lengths of different interactions rather than the interactions as just single units irrespective of time.

Discussion points

The standard differences that will have already occurred to you are of boys
and girls, different ethnic groupings, children with learning difficulties and
perceived differences in social class. Seating position in the room can be over-
looked easily as it is so much part of the given of the room. Less overt
differences are in terms of pupil's needs for attention and their shyness.

The need for teachers (and the department, corporately), to have well
planned lessons and schemes of work can be emphasized here. When pupil
activities are well defined, and within the skills of the pupils concerned, then
teachers are freer to behave pro-actively.

2.3b Interactions with Pupils

Student Teacher's Brief

In this activity you are to observe how science teachers distribute their
interactions across the cohort of pupils they are working with. The
allocation of time to individual pupils can become pupil driven as you
respond to pupil requests. As a professional you should try to have
more control over your actions. This means being more pro-active
than re-active. In classroom terms, you have to consciously distribute
your time across all pupils as equitably as your professional competence
allows.

Having collected data on other teachers you might usefully get
feedback on your behaviour from your mentor and colleagues. You
should use the information in the data to change your own pattern of
interactions.

Objective

Student teachers should improve the distribution of their interactions
with pupils as they become more aware of the interaction patterns of
themselves and others.

Instructions

- Sketch out a plan of the seating arrangements in the science class
  or laboratory in which you are observing. For example:

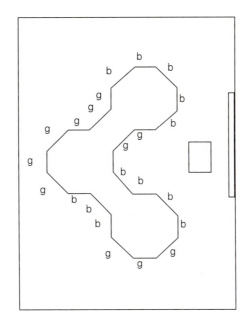

Figure 2.3: A sketch map of pupils' seating arrangements

- Mark on your plan identifications for pupils at different seating locations.

  If you know their names you could use initials. Boy/girl identifications will provide interesting data if used without names. You may use other forms of identification.

- Put a tally mark by the pupil the teacher interacts with each and every time there is an interaction.
- Look for patterns in the data you collect.
- Reflect on your own interactional patterns.
- Discuss this with your mentor.

2.4 Observing Pupils Learning

Mentor's Brief

Objective • Student teachers should be able to recognize possible ways in which different pupils have different educational experiences whilst in the same class.

Time • 2 or 3 lessons for student teacher's observations
  • $\frac{1}{2}$ hour discussion with mentor

Background

Student teachers, and experienced teachers too, have a 'responsibility escape clause' of pointing to pupil differences for contributing to differences in pupil learning. Student teachers can find it difficult to recognize that what pupils do in classrooms is, in part, due to what teachers do in classrooms. That is, the pupils are not completely and solely to blame. It is a cause for concern if a student teacher, who is in difficulties, denies any responsibility at all. It is a cause for alarm if the student teacher does not even realize there is anything wrong.

The intention of this activity is to provide student teachers with a structured opportunity to reflect on how their own practice could be improved to help more pupils learn more effectively and more efficiently. It is a matter of 'improved' and not 'made perfect'. For like the end of the rainbow, there is no such thing as perfect classroom practice. So student teachers should be helped to improve. They should be made to feel guilty if they can't be bothered.

Instructions

- Alert your colleagues to the observation activity.
- Brief the student teacher.
- Meet with the student teacher to discuss their findings and advice.

Discussion points

It is probably more effective if the student teacher can provide concrete examples of actions that are specific to the lessons observed. General advice is likely to be less useful than specific. If student teachers are to improve their own practice they must have clear ideas of which goals they are aiming to achieve in terms of their own actions. In the short term, small bits of behaviour are more achievable than long-term global ones. The reward of success with a small change can promote further change.

2.4 Observing Pupils Learning

Student Teacher's Brief

Pupils may be in the same class but this does not mean they have the same educational experiences or opportunities. It is not possible to get inside pupils' heads to find out what they are thinking. It *is* possible to record the actions they are engaged in. This observation task is about watching two different pupils, at the same time. The purpose of this is to reconsider how the planning, organization and management of

---

learning activities is crucial to providing better learning opportunities. This work can be used as a prelude to activity 9.5 on progression, differentiation, cognitive acceleration and pupil-differences.

Objective

You should be able to recognize possible ways in which different pupils have different educational experiences whilst in the same class.

Instructions

- Discuss suitable classes for observation with your mentor and colleagues.
- When you have selected classes, identify two pupils whose class-room performance is quite different.
- Sit in the class where you can see both pupils easily.
- You will need two separate recording sheets and a watch or small clock.
- Use the time-activity recording method from activity 4.1.
- At the end of the lesson, compare the time spent by the two pupils at different activities.
- Repeat with other pairs in other classes.

Consider the following questions.

- What differences were there in the activities of the two pupils?
- How did those differences arise?
- What responsibility lies with the teacher for those differences? Be as concrete as you can in terms of the teacher's actions, or lack of them.
- How could the teacher have organized activities differently to meet the different pupils' needs?
- Write out a set of points giving advice to yourself on the consequences of your findings.
- Discuss your findings and advice with your mentor.

2.5 Realising Aims

Mentor's Brief

Objective • Student teachers should be able to comment on how the wider aims of programmes of study might be realized.

Time   • 3 hours for student teacher's review of lessons and report writing.
           • ½ hour discussion with mentor.

Instructions

This activity should be tied in with the work in activity 4.5 and needs to precede it.

2.5 Realising Aims

Student Teacher's Brief

Grand aims are placed at the start of curriculum documents that set out programmes of study. These are very general and could often apply to any subject in the curriculum. The same aims have to be realized in classroom activities. The path from aim to activity can be obscure. You are asked to look at science lessons to see exactly *which* activities might add to the realization of which grand aims.

Objectives

You should be able to comment on how the wider aims of programmes of study might be realized in classroom activities.

Instructions

This set of grand aims is taken from the 1991 National Curriculum Council's non-statutory guidance.

'The following attitudes and personal qualities are important at all stages of science education:

curiosity
respect for evidence
willingness to tolerate uncertainty
critical reflection
perseverance
creativity and inventiveness
open-mindedness
sensitivity to the living and non-living environment
co-operation with others.

   • Review a scheme of work for a particular topic.
     Add to this your reflections on your own teaching and observations.

- For each of the attitudes and qualities listed in the quotation, write down at least one activity in the scheme of work that promoted that attitude or quality.
- Write a brief report on your findings.
- Use this information in your review of a scheme of work in activity 4.5.

Chapter 3

Activities for Pupils

Aims

If student teachers are to be able to choose activities for pupils, an essential part of their training must involve an introduction to a wide range of resources and strategies for the teaching of science. Choosing an activity also means being clear about the aims and objectives of lessons. Thus the aims of this chapter are:

- to provide an opportunity for student teachers to familiarize themselves with the equipment and resources available in the school for the teaching of science;
- to make student teachers aware of the importance of defining objectives for pupils;
- to introduce a range of different activities for the teaching of science;
- to consider criteria by which the selection of activities might be guided.

Introduction

Teaching is a complex activity, and as such, requires a diverse and comprehensive knowledge of resources and strategies, most of which are acquired incrementally over a lifetime's experience. These resources and strategies form the tools the teacher uses to help pupils to learn. It is important that student teachers become familiar with a basic repertoire of approaches. The time in a student teacher's training when they are likely to be most voracious in seeking and using different activities is when they take responsibility for planning, organizing and managing complete lessons for themselves. In activity 3.3, which should be planned for about such a time, alternatives are considered.

In preparation for that time, activity 3.1 requires the student teacher to become familiar with the resources in the science department. Consideration should be given to their effective use and the types of activities for pupils that might be developed.

Aims provide guiding constraints on the selection of activities for pupils. Student teachers often fail to see the importance of writing aims and objectives, particularly when many experienced teachers do not seem to plan lessons in this form. Four points need to be made here. Firstly, only the process of thoughtfully writing down objectives, for scrutiny and discussion, enables the student teacher to develop their knowledge of the form and variety of objectives. Secondly, this process generates the experienced teacher's skill of knowing the objectives without necessarily articulating them on paper. Thirdly, perhaps most importantly, is that the process of writing down objectives forces the student teacher to reflect on the purpose of the lesson in terms of learning. Failure to enter into this process often results in a lack of clarity in explaining to pupils what they have to do and why they are being asked to do it. Lacking an adequate explanation for both of these aspects, lessons can drift aimlessly with no apparent purpose or rationale. Fourthly, without objectives the student teacher will not have adequate criteria to judge the success of the lesson. So they are an essential component of lesson planning and must be insisted upon.

Activities 3.3 and 3.4 are an introduction to pupil activities that can facilitate learning. The emphasis is on activities for pupils other than the standard practical experiments that are a feature of most science courses. Aspects of investigations are discussed in Chapter 5. When pupils are asked the day after a practical science lesson, 'What did you do in science yesterday?', 'Why did you do it?' and 'What did you find out?', only a minority can answer these questions in a manner consistent with the teacher's aims for the lessons. This calls into question the value of relying solely on practical work for learning the ideas and theories of science. The development of scientific concepts requires science teachers to provide activities for children to interact with them. For example, the pupils might be involved in discussion, reading, analysing data or making models. These activities should be structured with clear objectives for pupils. The most important feature is that they require the pupil to be mentally active, processing and reflecting on the information. The time spent on activities can then be time well used rather than just being busy. Further writing activities for pupils are discussed in activity 6.3.

Finally, activity 3.5 is an opportunity to explore how learning activities should be matched to pupils' needs. In common with all the activities at the end of each chapter this student teacher activity offers opportunities for consolidation, reflection and wider professional development.

3.1 What Resources are Available for Pupils' Activities?

Mentor's Brief

Objective • Student teachers should know the resources the department has available and should be able to consider how they might be used.

Time
- For the student teacher, about 4 to 6 hours spread over a week
- 1 hour discussion with the mentor

Instructions

- Warn technicians and teaching staff that the student teacher will be asking questions about equipment and resources.
- Introduce this activity to the student teacher by stating that, as a professional, a teacher needs to know what resources they have to hand for organizing teaching and learning. Therefore it is the duty of any teacher new to a department to spend time finding out what resources are available.
- Direct the student teacher to the activity.
- Discuss the student teacher's answers.

3.1 What Resources are Available for Pupils' Activities?

Student Teacher's Brief

Objective

You should know the resources the department has available for the teaching of science and be able to consider how they might be used.

Instructions

- Follow the procedure set out below so as to familiarize yourself with the equipment and resources in the science department.
- Discuss your findings with your mentor.

Things to look for

Equipment

- Tour the main laboratories in which you will be teaching with a technician.
  Where are the following items stored?
  Bunsens, tripods, heat-proof mats, thermometers, glassware, Newtonmeters, microscopes, matches, glue, scissors and Sellotape, chemicals, power supplies, textbooks, subject specialist equipment.
- Where are the circuit breakers for the mains electricity, the master gas tap, fire extinguishers, fire blankets, first-aid kits, safety glasses, Hazcards?

- Is the equipment normally kept in locked cupboards?
  Can you have a key to get access to it if there is no technician available?
- For your own specialist subject, look through the cupboards of specialist apparatus.
     Is it all familiar to you?
     If not, how would you find out what it does and how to use it?
     Are there any obvious omissions in the equipment the school has?
     How are biological supplies organized?
     How is waste disposed of and what separations (glass, biological, other) are made?
- Where is the stationary kept?
     If a pupil needs a new book, can you just help yourself and hand it to him or her?
     What do you do if pupils say that they have lost a book?
     What is the procedure for obtaining chalk, white-board pens, OHP pens and acetates?

Textbooks/worksheets

- What textbooks does the school use for Key Stage 3?
- What textbooks does the school use for Key Stage 4?
- Do the children have a textbook each and are they allowed to take it home?
  If not, what resources if any, are available for setting homework?
- What worksheet schemes does the science department use?
     Where are these stored and what is the procedure for using them?
     How can additional copies be made?
- Does the department have additional texts for science-based activities e.g. SATIS, science readers, a small book-trolley.
- What range and quantity of science books are available in the school library?

Videos

- Does the department have a collection of videos? Where are they stored?
     What is the procedure for borrowing and returning them?
     Which ones in your specialist subject area are highly recommended by the other staff?
- If you would like a video recorded, what is the procedure?
- What is the system for ordering the video player for a lesson?

Information Technology

- Does the department have its own computers?
  What are they used for principally?
- Does the department have any of the following:
  Datalogging equipment?
  Software for Computer Assisted Learning (CAL)?
  CD-ROMs?
  In each case, how are they used in the classroom?
  Do you know how to use each of these? If not, how would you find out?
- What strategies are used for overcoming the problem that there may only be one computer in a class?

Posters/Classroom Displays

- Does the department have a collection of posters for display?
- Who is responsible for changing/maintaining the display in each classroom?
- Is it acceptable for the display areas to be used for samples of pupils' work?

3.2 Objectives for Pupils

Mentor's Brief

Objective
- Student teachers should be able to write behavioural objectives for pupils' activities.

Time
- 1 hour for the student teacher to review materials and write objectives
- $\frac{1}{2}$ hour for discussion with the mentor

Instructions

- Provide a range of material that forms the basis of typical lessons in your science department. These should include the following types of activity:
  Sc1 investigations
  Practical lessons introducing a new instrument, e.g. the ammeter or microscope
  Non-practical lessons using a resource such as textbooks or videos

Practical demonstrations

Circuses of practical activities

Class practical investigations on the relationship between two variables, e.g., force on a spring and its extension

Constructions of a simple model, e.g., a model of the heart or a planisphere

Introductions of a new idea, e.g., the distinction between solvents, solutes and solutions or the measurement of acceleration.

- Ask the student teacher to look at the lesson materials and then, for each lesson selected, to write possible learning objectives for pupils.
- Discuss the objectives for the activities with the student teacher.

Discussion points

- Was the process of writing objectives easy or difficult?
- Why might it be important that the pupils know what the purpose of the lesson is?
- Does writing objectives make it easier to explain what the purpose of the lesson is to the pupils?
- Do experienced teachers write objectives? If not, why not?

3.2 Objectives for Pupils

Student Teacher's Brief

Objective

You should be able to write objectives for pupils' activities.

Instructions

- Read the notes below on objectives.
- You have been provided with a number of standard science lessons which are commonly taught in this school.
- Read through the lesson material.
- Write out possible objectives for the pupils for the activities.
- Discuss with your mentor the objectives you have written.

Notes on objectives

Objectives are behavioural goals for pupils' activities and can be used as criteria by which learning can be measured. Thus an introductory lesson on electricity which has the aim 'to introduce the idea of simple circuits

---

and how they work', may have a set of objectives which are that pupils should be able to:

- construct a simple circuit with one battery and a bulb;
- explain how series circuits containing additional bulbs and batteries might be constructed.

These objectives focus attention on pupils' knowledge and their cognitive and manipulative skills. Typically, they include verbs such as 'recognize', 'state', 'explain', 'recall', 'draw', 'make', as these describe actions that are clearly achievable by pupils and define the objectives in terms of pupils' behaviour and actions. Descriptions of pupils' knowledge and skills with such words as 'understand' are too vague for behavioural objectives, although they may be suitable for aims.

There are big advantages in writing behavioural objectives as part of your lesson planning. Most importantly, it places the emphasis of lesson planning and delivery on the management of pupils' behaviour for the purpose of learning. It moves the focus from the teacher to the pupils who have to do the learning. This means it is easier for you, as a science teacher, to plan activities for pupils to give them the knowledge and the cognitive and manipulative skills that are your pupils' learning objectives. Behavioural objectives provide a useful yardstick for teachers to assess pupils and evaluate the lesson.

Aims can be confused with objectives. To avoid this confusion think of them as being found in different documents. Objectives belong in lesson plans. It is perhaps best to keep to aims in schemes of work. Aims are more general than objectives and are often written in looser, less behavioural language.

3.3 Extending the Repertoire of Pupils' Activities

Mentor's Brief

Objective • Student teachers should be able to draw upon an extended range of activities for pupils in drawing up lesson plans.

Time • Several hours of independent work for the student teacher
• Occasional discussions with the mentor

Background

Research shows that most student teachers start teaching by modelling or imitating activities suggested by their tutors, or those which they have personally experienced on a training course (Bennett and Carré, 1993). If they are not provided with a range of alternative pupil activities at this stage they may resort to the models they experienced in their own education. Student teachers should be encouraged to trial and evaluate as many pupil activities as possible and discuss their weaknesses and strengths. All individuals have to evolve their own teaching styles and they should be encouraged to do so by making reasoned and independent choices from their own experiences guided, rather than determined by, your experience.

This section considers how different pupil activities can be devised for use with the major resources used by science teachers:

- text
- video and
- information technology.

Pupils' work in creative writing and issues of language are dealt with in more detail in Chapter 6. This can be extended to art work, although this is not discussed in Chapter 6. Field-trips, museum visits and visiting speakers all provide alternative activities for pupils. These are touched on in Chapter 7. Role-playing and drama have an immediate place in considering education about science, particularly in historical and ethical work and this is discussed in Chapter 8.

Instructions

- The student teacher should be directed to the activities 3.3a, b and c.
- Explain that the tasks to be carried out will need discussion after their completion.

Discussion points

- In your discussion with the student teacher on the pupils' activities, add as many new and different examples as you can, including activities you may not personally use, so as to help build the student teacher's repertoire.

3.3a Directed Activities Related to Texts

Student Teacher's Brief

Objective

From different textual resources you should be able to construct DARTs (directed activities related to texts) activities for pupils.

Instructions

- Read the notes and examples of DARTs below.
- Construct 3 DARTs of your own for specific lessons and topics.
- Discuss them with your mentor along with your lesson plans.
- Trial the DARTs in lessons.
- Discuss the outcomes with your mentor.

Notes on DARTs

Essentially there are two types of DARTs — those which require the text to be reconstructed and those which require the text to be analysed. Students need to be introduced to both types and shown samples of each.

Reconstruction DARTs

There are four principal types of reconstruction DARTs:

- text completion;
- diagram completion;
- table completion;
- reconstruction of a disordered text.

Text completion DARTs can involve pupils adding appropriate words in the blanks that have been left in a previously complete text. This type of activity is often known as a CLOZE procedure and is popular in areas outside science. In both diagram completion and table completion DARTs, pupils add labels to a diagram or complete a table. The reconstruction of a disordered text is most useful where there is a logical sequence or structure in the text. Descriptions of experimental procedures, descriptions of anatomical structures and procedures in time generally are suitable for this treatment.

Analysis DARTs

There are five different types of analysis DARTs:

- underlining text;
- labelling text;
- summarizing with a diagram;
- summarizing with a table;
- writing questions about a text.

Underlining involves pupils scanning a text searching for relevant key words, concepts or related ideas. Labelling text would require pupils to add headings or labels for paragraphs so as to produce a form of telegraphic summary. Both diagrammatic and tabular representations can be constructed for ideas, concepts or data. These involve pupils translating information from one form to another. A question-writing DART would require pupils to construct their own questions. See activity 10.4 for more details on pupils writing questions.

Examples of DARTs

A text completion DART
[Instructions to pupils]
Do the following task as a pair.
Read the passage and fill in the missing words.
Carry out the activities at the end.

The Distinction between Mass and Weight

In common speech we often say things like 'This bag of sugar weighs one _____'. As we shall see, '_____' has a different meaning to a scientist.

The quantity we are talking about when we measure out one kilogram of sugar is the amount of sugar that we have. This is what scientists refer to as the mass of sugar. Mass is measured in _____ and is a measure of the reluctance of an object to change its motion, what is called its _____.

The _____ of an object is something quite different. Everything is attracted to the Earth by _____. This is referred to as the 'force of _____'. That is exactly what gravity is, a force. Forces are measured in _____. Gravity is supposed to have been discovered by Sir Isaac Newton when an apple fell on his head; a nice story. The weight of a body is a measure of the _____ with which _____ attracts it to the _____, and as a force it is measured in Newtons.

The confusion between mass and weight arises because the force with which the Earth attracts a body is directly proportional to the _____. That is to say the more _____ the more weight. This provides us with a convenient way of measuring mass. Two masses can be compared by placing them on opposite arms of a balance. If one has greater mass than the other then the force of gravity on it will be stronger and the beam will be _____ of _____. If the two masses are equal then the weight will be the same and the beam will balance.

In effect, we compare masses by comparing _____. This is the origin of expressions like 'I have weighed these apples and they weigh three kilograms'.

Modern weighing machines no longer compare weights. They measure weights using spring devices which have been pre-calibrated. A device can be set up to give a reading in kilograms. All equal masses have the same _____. This means that if you measure this weight you can work back to find out the mass.

Think back to those films of men walking on the surface of the Moon. It really was a strange new world wasn't it? It was almost as if things were happening in slow motion.

The reason for this is that the force with which the Moon's gravity attracts objects is much _____ than that of the Earth. That's why, even without air resistance, things fall more slowly on the Moon.

Things weigh _____ on the Moon than they do on Earth. It is a terrific, but very expensive way of losing weight. Unfortunately the effect is not long lasting because although we weigh less on the Moon our _____ remains unchanged so on return to Earth we weigh the same.

- Now re-read the text and write a heading above or beside each paragraph, e.g. for the first paragraph, you may well put the heading 'Common use of the word weight.'
- Now underline all those sentences which tell you something about mass.
- Now double underline, or use a different colour all those sentences which tell you something about weight.
- When you have finished write a few sentences, describing what you think is the difference between mass and weight.

Consider which words are the words to remove: scientific word, verbs, conjunctions?
Why is it essential that pupils should do these tasks in pairs?
Discuss this with your mentor.

A disordered text DART
In constructing one of these, it is important that lines of text are scrambled before it is printed so that pupils cannot use edge-joins as clues to the correct order.

Investigating the Relationship between Acceleration and Force

[Instructions for pupils]
Cut the instructions for steps in an experiment into strips.
Rearrange the strips to give the correct sequence of steps for the experiment.
Paste the correct sequence into your book.

Mark out the strip into divisions of 'ten-ticks'.
Label the first one A, the second one B and so on.

Connect the ticker-timer to a 12V power supply.

Draw up a graph with two axes, time and speed in cm/t.t.

Now calculate the acceleration using the formula
acc. = change is speed ÷ time taken.

Friction compensates the slope so that the trolley maintains a steady speed as it rolls down the hill (the dots should keep the same separation all the time).

Measure the difference in height between the strip A and strip F, 6 'ten-ticks' later. This is the difference in speed between the two.

Now accelerate the trolley with one elastic band.
Remember to attach a new tape and turn on the timer.

Set up the ramp so that there is a slight incline.

Paste the first 'ten-tick' in adjacent to the y axis.
Paste strip B next to it and so on till you have at least 6 strips on your graph.

Repeat this procedure for two elastic bands and three elastic bands.
Attach a tape to the trolley.

Teachers commenting on this technique have said that although it takes an extra five minutes to do this procedure at the start of an experiment, it results in a much more efficient use of time by the pupils, with the experiment being carried out much more effectively. Consider why you think this might be so.

An underlining, analysis DART
The third type of DART here is an analysis DART. It requires pupils to read and re-read the text using the techniques of underlining and table construction to summarize the text.

Solids, liquids and gases

[Instructions to pupils]

- First read the whole passage with care.
- With a coloured pencil, underline the parts of the passage which tell you about the movement of the particles.

- Now double-underline those parts of the passage which tell you about compressing or squashing a substance.
- Using the headings, 'Solid', 'Liquid' and 'Gas', make a table which summarizes how particles move
- Use the same headings to make a table which summarizes how easy it is to compress a substance.

The most obvious feature of the way that the particles are arranged in a substance depends on whether it is a solid, a liquid or a gas.

The particles in a solid must be held in fixed positions, otherwise solids would not retain their shapes. Moreover, the particles in a solid must be packed very tightly together. This is evident from the fact that solids are very difficult to compress. Even at very high pressures, the change in volume is very small indeed.

In most liquids, the particles are less tightly packed than in a solid. This is evident when a solid is melted as there is usually an increase in volume on the change from solid to liquid. However, since liquids are also difficult to compress, the particles must still be very close together. The main difference between solids and liquids is that liquids have no shape. They take the shape of the container and are free to move about and can be poured. Obviously, the particles in a liquid are not fixed in any definite position. They are able to move about, rolling over each other like grains of sand.

Gases not only take up the shape of the vessel which contains them but also spread out to occupy the whole vessel. This is easily seen by using a coloured gas like bromine. Our picture of a gas is one in which the particles are free to move about and there are quite large spaces between them. Increasing the pressure on a gas brings the particles closer together. If this increase in pressure is large enough then the particles become as close together as in a liquid. The gas will then change into a liquid.

3.3b Using Videos

Student Teacher's Brief

A typical educational video is in the order of twenty minutes duration. Even an extract of five minutes is generally packed with a high density of information. However interesting, watching it is a passive experience. The design problem for lesson planning to incorporate the use of video is to design activities that make pupils active, not passive.

Objective

You should be able to select different ways of using videoed material with classes and incorporate your selection into a lesson as a pupil activity.

Instructions

- Read the notes on strategies for using videos below.
- Produce your own list of a range of approaches.
  Add notes on possible advantages and disadvantages for each method.
- Plan an activity for pupils using a video in a lesson you will teach.
- Discuss the plan with your mentor.
- Teach the lesson and evaluate the activity.
- Discuss the evaluation with your mentor.

Notes on strategies for using videos

Some of the strategies that may emerge in the discussion are:

- Providing a list of questions about the video which pupils must complete after watching it.
- Breaking the video after several minutes to discuss the issue raised before going onto the next section.
- Asking pupils to write a one paragraph summary of what the video was about, in pairs. Follow this by getting one or two to read out their summaries to the rest of the class.
- Breaking the pupils into four groups, A–D. Group A are told that they will have to produce a one paragraph summary of the first five minutes, group B the second five minutes and so on. At the end of the video, each group is given five–ten minutes to produce the summary and then the groups are mixed so that there is one person from each group in the new groups. The groups now pool their summaries to produce a composite summary which is no longer than one page. This is then reproduced by the teacher for the whole group. Although lengthy, this is an effective means of getting children to summarize a video.
- Providing a diagram which can be annotated from the information in the video. This is particularly useful for anything that involves descriptions of body parts or mechanisms. The parts have to be labelled and then notes added explaining the function.
- Producing a poster summary. This method is useful for videos dealing with topical issues, e.g. pollution and nuclear power. Pupils can be asked to produce posters which show the problems and possible solutions, advantages and disadvantages or different methods of tackling the problem.

3.3c   Using Information Technology

Student Teacher's Brief

Objectives

You should become more familiar with the school's IT provision and be able to plan to include IT in your lessons.

Background

Science education should be an opportunity to learn to use the tools and instruments of the scientist. This is the justification used for teaching children how to use a Bunsen burner, a thermometer and an oscilloscope. These days, instrumentation for many scientists is linked to information technology — both for the collection of data and its analysis and interpretation. A science education which does not provide children with opportunities to experience such use is inevitably incomplete. Information technology can enable science teaching to transcend the constraints imposed on experimental work by a school laboratory and periods of study of approximately an hour in length. IT instruments enable phenomena to be studied which happen very rapidly, e.g. record a microphone trace, or events which happen over much greater periods of time, e.g. the growth of a plant. It has been shown clearly that the opportunity to see the graphical representation of an event *as it is happening* significantly improves pupils' cognitive skills with scientific representation.

Instructions

- Conduct an audit of your skills by rating your ability to use the following packages.

	Poor	Fair	Good
Databases	......	....	....
Word-processing	......	....	....
Spreadsheets	......	....	....
Other software	......	....	....

- Ask your mentor who is responsible for IT across the curriculum.
  Discuss with your mentor what IT provision there is in the science department and how you can become more skilled in using it.
- Practice with the IT software and data logging so that you are skilled in using it.

- Consider opportunities for introducing IT into your lessons.
- Plan such lessons.
- Teach using the IT.
- Discuss the outcomes with your mentor.

For further reading on this subject see, *The IT in Secondary Science Book: A compendium of ideas for using information technology in science* by Roger Frost (1994), London: IT in Science.

3.4 Pupils' Activities with Concepts

Mentor's Brief

Objective
- Student teachers should be able to introduce into lessons activities that require pupils to articulate their concepts and ideas in science topics.

Time
- 2 hours for the student teacher to carry out the activities and reflect on their use
- $1/2$ hour discussion with mentors

Background

This student teacher activity explores the use of concept maps and allied techniques. This is a generic activity which can be used in most areas of the curriculum as a means of articulating conceptual knowledge. There is evidence to show that their regular use produces a significant improvement in pupils' understanding of science (Horton, 1992). One of the important features of concept mapping, and other activities described here, is that they make pupils talk about and clarify their own scientific knowledge through discussion with other pupils. Traditionally, such opportunities are rarely provided in many classes. The other pupil activities are variants on this strategy which encourage pupils to think about the appropriate use of scientific language and the meaning of scientific terms.

Instructions

- As with any activity, it is best if tried first, so the student teacher should be asked to make a concept map. She should also try the other activities of word association and key sentences.
- Discuss the student teacher's experiences with the activities and her reflections on how the activities might best be incorporated into schemes of work and lesson plans.

Discussion points

Raise these questions in your discussion with the student teacher:

- Which is more important — the final product or the process of producing it?
- What are the features of this activity which make it a potentially valuable learning experience?
- When would it be most appropriate to use this activity?

3.4 Pupils' Activities with Concepts

Student Teacher's Brief

Objective

You should be able to introduce into lessons activities that require pupils to articulate their concepts and ideas in science topics.

Instructions

- Carry out the activities that are described below.
- Answer the questions for reflection at the end of each activity.
- Consider how these activities might be built into a scheme of work.
- Discuss your reflections with your mentor.

Activities for articulating concepts

Concept mapping
Concept mapping is a technique which sees words essentially as labels for concepts or ideas and asks individuals to define the relationships between them. Typically, a list of words is provided, e.g.

Nebula	Galaxy	Star	Meteor
Comet	Planet	Ursa Major	Solar system
Satellite	Universe	Red shift	Red giant
White dwarf	Black hole	Meteosat	Shooting star
Andromeda	Constellation		

The following instructions are then given to group of 3–4 pupils.

- Write each of the above words in large letters on a small piece of squared paper (4 cm × 4 cm).
- Sort the squares into two piles — those you know the meaning of and those you do not understand.
- Discard the pile of words you do not understand.

- Now lay out the remaining words on a large piece of poster paper. Place those words that are related adjacent to each other.
- When you are happy with the arrangement, stick the squares down.
- Draw lines between the terms that are connected.
- Now add a few words or a sentence to the lines to explain how they are connected.
  For instance

UNIVERSE – – – –▶– – – – STARS
consists of

- When you have finished pin your map up for others to look at.

Now, answer these questions:

- What value would it have for learning?
- How could it be used in other areas of the curriculum?
- How often and where should it be used in a topic?

Word Association

For this technique, you are asked to think of all the words that you associate with a particular word in the order that they come into your mind. It is particularly useful for words that represent key concepts in science. Try it yourself for the following words. Write the key word and then the *first ten* words that you associate with it, e.g. Photosynthesis, Oxidation or Energy. When you have finished, write a sentence which states the relationship between the key word and each of the ten words that you associate with it.

Now, answer these questions:

- What might be the educational value of this activity?
- What would be a good method of using it?
- Should it be done on an individual basis or by pairs of pupils? Why?

Key Sentences

This technique is essentially another variation on the theme of word association and typically the activity takes 30–40 minutes.

Pupils are provided with a list of key words which have a scientific meaning and an everyday meaning. Such a list for energy with GCSE pupils could be

energy	kinetic	lost
transfer	electricity	heating

potential	conservation	insulator
conductor	sound	light
work	joules	Newton
force	metre	stored

Instructions to pupils:

- On your own write five sentences.
  Each sentence must contain at least two of the words in the above list.
- Now join with three others. Share your sentences with them and discuss whether your sentences are scientifically correct.
- In your group, pick five sentences, three of which you are sure are scientifically correct and two which you are not sure about. Write these on a piece of paper.
- Pass the sheet to the group next to you on your left. With the sheet that is passed to you, discuss as a group whether you think each sentence is scientifically correct. If you think so, mark it with a tick. If not, mark it with a cross.
- When you have finished pass your piece of paper onto the next group.
  Continue this till your piece of paper returns to you.

Now, answer these questions:

- What is the focus of the strategy for learning in activities such as concept mapping, word association and key sentences?
- Why might this be of value?
- When would it be of value?

3.5 Selecting Appropriate Activities

Mentor's Brief

Objective • The student teacher should be able to select activities to match pupils' needs and give an adequate rationale for their choice.

Time • 2 hours for the student teacher to carry out the activities and reflect on their use
• $\frac{1}{2}$ hour discussion with mentor

Background

Studies by Her Majesty's Inspectorate (HMI) have consistently shown that the ability of teachers to match tasks to children is generally poor: the requirements of high attainers are underestimated and low attainers overestimated. Student teachers should now have sufficient experience of a range of pupils' activities in the classroom to begin the process of thinking about the issues involved in the matching of activity to pupil performance.

The broader issues, expressed in a programme of study, need translating into schemes of work and then into classroom practice and pupil activities at the level of the lesson plan. Global aims, individual pupil performance and skills, as well as the constraints of the individual science department, all influence how the selection of pupils' activities is made.

Work in activity 2.5 on realizing aims and that in 9.5 on differentiation may be particularly relevant and helpful to this activity. Activity 3.5 should be carried out before activity 4.5, on revising part of a scheme of work, which can be used as an umbrella for these other activities.

Instructions

- Direct the student teacher to the two grids in the student teachers' activity.
- Discuss with the student teacher his or her report on the questions at the ends of the grids.

3.5   Selecting Appropriate Activities

Student Teacher's Brief

Objective

You should be able to select pupils' activities to match pupils' needs by considering criteria that you can articulate.

Instructions

- Carry out the activities that are described below.
- Answer the questions for reflection at the end of each activity.
- Write a brief report on your answers to the questions at the ends of the activities with the two grids.
- Discuss your report with your mentor.

An aims/activity grid

- Work through the grid and enter a tick where the activity is suitable for that aim and a cross where it would be unsuitable.
- Now use the final column. Put an O in the column if you have

---

used that kind of activity often, a N if you have never used that activity and an S if you have used that technique sometimes.

Table 3.1: An aims/activity grid

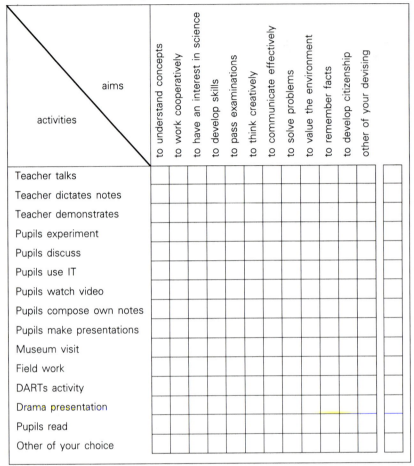

activities \ aims	to understand concepts	to work cooperatively	to have an interest in science	to develop skills	to pass examinations	to think creatively	to communicate effectively	to solve problems	to value the environment	to remember facts	to develop citizenship	other of your devising	
Teacher talks													
Teacher dictates notes													
Teacher demonstrates													
Pupils experiment													
Pupils discuss													
Pupils use IT													
Pupils watch video													
Pupils compose own notes													
Pupils make presentations													
Museum visit													
Field work													
DARTs activity													
Drama presentation													
Pupils read													
Other of your choice													

- Now look carefully at the profile that you have just completed. What does it tell you about your approach to teaching?
- Is there a good reason why you have made little use of some of these activities?
- Are there any rules for deciding which activities are suitable for which aims?
  What might those rules be?
- How do different activities for pupils promote different images of the nature of science?
- Which image do you wish to promote?
- How should you change your teaching?

Enjoying science

- Check, with a tick, those things which may be particularly enjoyed by the groups listed. Put a cross for activities that you judge to be inappropriate for particular groups.

Table 3.2: *A pupil activity/enjoyment grid*

Which activities do you think pupils will enjoy? (Tick those which you think would be particularly successful.)	11-yr-old boys of high ability	11-yr-old co-ed unstreamed	13-yr-old girls average ability	15-yr-old co-ed top GCSE group	16-yr-old school leavers	first-yr sixth form
Doing an experiment described on a workcard						
Watching a teacher demonstration						
Writing notes from dictation for 15 min.						
Composing own notes for 15 min.						
Taking part in a small group work on the design of an experiment						
Listening to a 20-minute talk from the teacher on a topic from the syllabus						
Copying a diagram from a book						
Participating in a class discussion on the importance of discovery in science						
Preparing a display or exhibition						
Reading an article from a magazine						

- Which activity do you judge to be the most universally applicable? Why might this be so?

- Which activity do you judge to be the least universally applicable? Again, why might this be so?
- Are there patterns across the activities and groups of pupils in terms of enjoyment? What are these patterns?
- Are there any rules for deciding which activities pupils might enjoy?
  What are they?

Chapter 4

Planning and Managing

Aims

Teachers are managers. They may be managers of more than thirty learners at a time. The teachers don't do the learning in the way that a factory manager doesn't actually operate the machines in the factory. The teacher, as manager, does have a responsibility to make sure that the learners can 'manufacture' their learning. The aims of the activities in this chapter are to help student teachers to develop the following:

- knowledge of the elements of planning and classroom management;
- skills and strategies for organizing and managing activities in lessons;
- skills and strategies in planning and managing continuity between lessons;
- experience in developing and planning a scheme of work.

Introduction

In this chapter, the focus is on the *how* of teaching: procedures, routines and strategies. This is closely linked with Chapter 3, where the focus is on the *what* of teaching: what is available and which activities might be selected. Student teachers need to see the symbiosis of these.

Activity 4.1 introduces the lesson plan as the basic document that supports teachers while they are at work. The lesson plan combines how things are to be done, with the choice of what is to be done. Student teachers need to be directed to producing lesson plans that are clear, coherent and concise. This should help them build repertoires of procedures, routines and strategies. Activity 4.1 introduces lesson plans as support documents. The selection of classroom activities for lesson plans will, in the main, be for pupil activities. It is therefore important that the student teachers think about what the pupils will get from the activities as well as how to organize and manage the activities themselves. What are the pupils 'manufacturing', in terms of their knowledge and skills, through the operation of that particular learning activity? This ties in with activity 3.2 on objectives for pupils.

The activities for student teachers in 4.2 are intended to help student teachers develop skills in teaching parts of lessons. The recommended strategy for mentors is to introduce the student teacher to planning, organizing and managing these smaller parts of lessons before the student teacher graduates to teaching a complete lesson unassisted. Student teachers will need to be able to plan sections of lessons in more detail than appears on the standard lesson plan. Where a key skill, piece of knowledge, use of a scientific tool or technique is to be introduced auxiliary prompts and directions should be developed during planning. The directions on 'observation with a higher resolution' in activity 2.2 should help student teachers see the consequences of other teachers' decisions over choices of sequencing and pupil activity. Activity 4.3 is directed at the planning, organizing and managing of complete lessons.

Activities 4.4 and 4.5 are designed for use when student teachers take responsibility for teaching a complete topic area in a programme of study. Student teachers should be required to review and revise part of a scheme of work for a module, unit or topic. This is planning, organizing and managing the largest unit of work that a student teacher might reasonably be expected to deal with. Mentors should select some topic in need of revision and/or development. The product of this revision should be useful to all members of the department and therefore needs to be as close to full professional standards as possible. In this way, the student teacher can become yet further incorporated into the working of the science department by sharing in its corporate responsibilities. The focus of their attention can be directed to the objectives, activities, assessments, coherence and continuity of the scheme of work for that topic. Issues of the openness of the activities (Chapter 5), the development of the learner's language skills (Chapter 6) and the nature of differentiation and progression (Chapter 9) should start to play a more prominent and integrated part of the student teacher's planning.

Most student teachers are anxious about classroom control. They can be reassured if their work is presented as a management job rather than a performance job. Planning, organizing and managing effectively can considerably reduce the opportunities for classroom disruption. Pupils can be expected to be on-task when their tasks are well-planned and well-organized.

4.1 Elements of a Lesson Plan

Mentor's Brief

Objective • Student teachers should be able to list the elements of a lesson plan, comment on their necessity in supporting the teacher as a manager and comment on the advantages and disadvantages of different styles of lesson plan.

Time   • 1 hour of student teacher time
         • $\frac{1}{2}$ hour discussion with mentor

Instructions

   • Provide the student teacher with various lesson plans. If a variety of
     different styles can be used from your own stock this would be an
     advantage.
   • Give the student teacher time to answer the questions in the activity
     brief.
   • Meet to discuss the student teacher's answers.

Discussion points

   • Key elements of a lesson plan include:
            date;
            class;
            time and room, for record keeping and reference purposes.
   • Some indication should be made to the:
            topic, module, or referenced scheme of work;
            specific lesson topic, or scheme of work reference.
   • The bulk of the plan should concentrate on:
            objectives for general orientation;
            activities for the pupils;
            estimates of the time each activity will take;
            some indication of the real time at which activities might be
              expected to start;
            short experimental notes and safety warnings;
            sizes of pupils' working groups together with the number of
              groups;
            book references and key questions, homework.

With a range of different styles, advantages, disadvantages and additions are
easier to highlight and discuss. The principle differences are likely to be in
terms of managerial guidance on sub-sections of the lesson, e.g. in the lesson
plan given below, the notes for the pupils to copy down from the board
might be explicitly written out in advance rather than made up on the spur
of the moment. Similarly the summary for the lesson might be worked out
in advance. A written reminder on which microscope objective to use would
be helpful. A safety warning card for the ammonia and hydrochloric acid
experiment and perhaps the boiling kettle will be essential. Other points will
doubtless emerge as you draw upon your own experience and expertise.

4.1   Elements of a Lesson Plan

Student Teacher's Brief

Objective

You should be able to list the elements of a lesson plan, comment on their necessity in supporting the teacher as a manager and comment on the advantages and disadvantages of different styles of lesson plan.

Instructions

- Look at the lesson plans provided by your mentor together with the example below.
- Write down what you think are the key elements of a lesson plan.
- Note down why those elements are necessary.
- Briefly note down how lesson plans might differ.
- Think of the advantages and disadvantages of different styles of lesson plan.
- List other paper-support materials (not worksheets for the pupils) you might need to prepare to help you organize and manage the pupils' learning. Why might you need them?

Specimen lesson plan

Group 10c   Week 6
Wednesday, 2 June   10 am Lab. 2

Topic:	The macroscopic properties of materials and their micro-scopic structure.
Lesson:	Brownian motion and the particulate nature of matter.
Objectives:	Pupils should be able to:

- use the particulate model of matter to explain some physical phenomena;
- follow instructions to observe Brownian motion in smoke.

Real time	*Activities*	*Time taken in minutes*
10.00	Entry/register/collect lab reports on size of oil molecule.	5
10.05	(safety warnings)	
	Q. 'What is happening here?'	
	Point out two sets of stations: 4 people per station.	
	Circus of activities on particulate matter:	

	boiling kettle and melting ice-cubes/permanganate crystals in water	
	smell of scent/fuming of ammonia and hydrochloric acid.	
	Pupils to circulate and note down what they observe.	15
10.20	Collect pupils' own descriptions and ideas and write them on the board.	10
10.30	Pupils copy down summary notes from board: particles/motion/temperature.	10
10.40	Brownian motion experiment (Bk. 1. p. 51. expt. 5) pupil to read instructions aloud from the book. Discuss.	10
10.50	Do Brownian motion experiment in groups of 3 (10 microscopes).	15
11.05	Pupils start write up with diagram of smoke cell.	15
11.15	Summarize the morning's activities. Home assignment of experimental write up and photocopied GCSE question p. 1. Q6.	5
11.20	End.	

4.2 Team-teaching Parts of Lessons

Mentor's Brief

Objective • Student teachers should be able to use a variety of teaching skills and strategies in a team-teaching situation.

Time • Lesson time, and up to 2 hours for the student teacher on each activity to be planned, discussed, organized, taught and reviewed.
• Lesson time, and up to $\frac{1}{2}$ hour for the discussion of the plan, observation and debrief with mentor.

Background

Four learning opportunities for pupils have been selected for student teachers to develop their planning, organizational and classroom management skills:

  4.2a   Pencil and paper task
  4.2b   Class practical
  4.2c   Demonstration with a question and answer routine
  4.2d   Explanation at the board with a question and answer routine

The tasks, and the order in which they are presented here, are graded in terms of the amount of direct classroom control the student teacher must assume.

It is far easier to manage a well-defined pencil and paper task than to manage a question and answer routine while dealing with some explanation at the board. Generally the more the pupils are on-task, independently of the student teacher, the easier it will be to manage that learning opportunity.

Activity 4.2b, 'Class practical', and activity 6.2a, 'Eliciting ideas' compliment each other as do activity 4.2c, 'Demonstration with a question and answer routine' and 6.2b, 'Sharing ideas'.

Instructions

For each activity:

- Select opportunities for the student teacher to team-teach parts of lessons with you, with colleagues, or with other student teachers.
- Brief the student teacher well before the day of the lesson.
- Discuss the student teacher's preparation in advance of the lesson.
- Select an observation technique from the activities in Chapter 2.
  Use this when the student teacher teaches.
- Team-teach the lesson. When the student teacher is teaching, observe the student teacher's actions.
  Record your observations.
- Debrief the student teacher by asking for their thoughts on their actions.
  Make your opening comments positive.
  Where actions can be improved focus on the specific action and demonstrate in the room, there and then, if possible. (Refer to Chapter 1: Action 3, Debriefing.)

Discussion points

- Managerial issues that might arise include:
  timing
  grouping of pupils
  moving of pupils to better places for visibility
  positioning of the student teacher themselves and monitoring of all corners of the room by scanning and the student teacher's own movement around the room
  organizing of resources in terms of positioning for access
  distribution and collection
  availability of all the resources required
  light, ventilation and heat levels would be a joint team responsibility at this stage.
- Pedagogic issues include:
  appropriateness of the language level
  repetition and display of new words and ideas

elicitation of pupils' own ideas

appropriate selection of activities to match the learning objectives.

- Content issues include:

  coherence of the science

  appropriateness of the science to the topic and everyday life

  use of evidence and the ways in which we know what we know

  development of examples or the explanation of techniques.

- Performance issues include:

  body posture

  eye contact with the members of the class

  voice level and variation

  pacing of speech

  use of chalkboard or OHP

  the checking that board writing can be seen by all.

4.2a   Pencil and Paper Activity

Student Teacher's Brief

This is the first of four activities that are designed to help you learn and
practise teaching skills. The teaching activities are all parts of lessons
rather than a complete lesson. The intention is that you will benefit from
observing your team-teaching partner at work as well as having their
support when you come to organize and manage your activity in the
lesson. Your partner can observe your actions and provide you with
feedback.

Objective

You should be able to plan, organize and manage a pencil and paper
activity.

Instructions

Refer to activity 6.2b.

In planning your part in the lesson you need to do the following:

- Briefly discuss the task with your mentor or the class teacher.
- Locate the task materials or resources.
- Think about how the task fits into the general pattern of the
  lesson.

  Decide upon pupil objectives for the task: what the pupils
  will be able to do or know that they could not do or didn't
  know beforehand.

> Decide on timings: how long do you estimate the task to take?

- Find out or decide about:
  > the expendability and need for duplication of worksheets
  > number of texts and sharing (books)
  > the status of the writing (rough, best, to be corrected, assessed etc.)
  > the initial instructions to pupils, write them out to clarify them for yourself
  > the final instructions to pupils.
- Discuss the lesson plan with your team-teaching partner.
- Supplement the lesson plan with notes for your activity.
- Do the pencil and paper task for yourself so you know exactly what the pupils will be doing.

These are things you should do during the time that you take charge:

- Check that pupils have understood your instructions (ask someone to repeat them back to you).
- Check that the pupils understand the purpose of the task and how it fits into the lesson.
- Monitor the pupils' progress on the task by circulating around the room and checking their work.
- Keep a watch on the time.
- Decide on when to warn the pupils that they will be stopping soon.
- Stop the pupils.
- Ask one or two pupils to tell the class their answers, discuss the results or summarize for the pupils.
- Hand over to your colleague ready for the next activity.

4.2b   Class Practical

Student Teacher's Brief

Objective

You should be able to plan, organize and manage a class practical as part of a lesson.

Instructions

This activity is complimented by activity 6.2a, 'Eliciting pupils' ideas'. In planning your part in the lesson you need to do the following:

- Briefly discuss the class practical with your mentor or team-teaching partner.
- Think about how the practical is part of the scheme of work.
    Decide which process skills are to be emphasized or assessed.
    Decide on the content knowledge the experiment develops.
    Decide how the experiment exemplifies the scientific approach.
    Decide if the experiment is to be exploratory, hypothesis testing or illustrative.
- Write out behavioural objectives for the pupils' learning.
- Decide about the following:
    grouping of learners: pairs or threes (with fours there will always be one person who is not immediately next to the person doing the experiment at that moment);
    how much of everything will you need for the number of groups that will operate;
    timings: how long do you estimate the experiment to take;
    safety and COSSH requirements;
    where in the laboratory items will be placed for access by pupils;
    disposal of waste and used materials.
- Practise the experiment so you know what advice to give pupils so they will be successful in the task.
- Discuss your plan for the class practical with your team-teaching partner.

These are things you should organize before your activity in the lesson:

- Order the equipment from the technicians within their deadline.
- Check on the experimental instructions to pupils for completeness, correctness, safety aspects and the number of copies required.
- Check on the nature of the pupils' written reports: rough, best, to be marked, assessed and so on.

Before the lesson you need to check on the following:

- That the technicians have prepared your equipment for the laboratory.
- The position of equipment/chemicals/samples for orderly collection by pupils.
- Count items that might be lost or easily removed from the laboratory and keep a note of how many there are.

When you take charge of the class experiment you should pay attention to the following:

- Give out worksheets if they are to be used. Rehearse with the class what they will do and why, providing the focus is not one of following written instructions.
- Point out safety issues.
- Organize the orderly collection of equipment/chemicals/samples.
- Circulate amongst groups when pupils are experimenting. Ask probing questions about the purpose of the practical, their observations, conclusions, justifications. (See activity 6.2a.)
- Trouble-shoot problems of specific groups.
- Keep a general watchful eye on the progress of groups you are not immediately dealing with (you will not need eyes in the back of your head just a general scanning strategy).
- To give further instructions, call pupils to order when necessary and insist on silence.
- Give pupils a warning of imminent finishing and clearing away.
- Supervise the orderly return, and counting back, of equipment.
- Supervise the disposal of waste.
- Return the class's attention to your team-teaching partner.

4.2c Demonstration with Question and Answers

Student Teacher's Brief

Objective

You should be able to plan, organize and manage a demonstration.

Instructions

This activity is complimented by activity 6.2b, 'Sharing ideas'.
In planning your part in the lesson you need to do the following:

- Briefly discuss the task with your mentor, the class teacher or your team-teaching partner.
- Find out which demonstration to do.
- Think about how the activity fits into the general pattern of the lesson.
  > Decide on pupil objectives for the demonstration in terms of both pupils' process skills and content knowledge.
  > Decide on timings: how long do you estimate the demonstration to take?

- Find out or decide about:
    which apparatus/chemicals/samples you need;
    where these are kept, which cupboards;
    how the apparatus fits together, what the procedure is;
    safety and COSSH requirements.
  Discuss these with the technicians.
- Practise all demonstrations before you do them with a class.
- Discuss your plan for the demonstration with your team-teaching partner.

These are things you should organize before your activity in the lesson:

- Order the equipment from the technicians within their deadline.
- Decide upon where in the laboratory is the best place to do the demonstration so that all will be able to see clearly and safely. Decide on key questions to focus the pupils' attention on the phenomenon and their ideas about it.
- Check that everything you need is ready in the laboratory.
- Briefly check the arrangements with your team-teaching partner.

During the time that you take charge of the demonstration you need to do the following.

- Group the pupils around the demonstration. Ensure that all can see clearly.
- Mention safety if necessary.
- Elicit pupils' ideas on what is present on the bench. (See activity 6.2b.)
- Elicit pupils' ideas about what will happen, or does happen.
- Ask your questions two or three times before choosing a respondent.
- Nominate respondents across different groups (boys – girls, front – back, those with hands up – those without, etc.).
- Watch the clock so you don't over-run.
- Summarize what they have seen and discussed.
- Return people to their places in an orderly fashion ready for the next activity.

4.2d Explanation at the Board or OHP

Student Teacher's Brief

Objective

You should be able to plan, organize and manage an explanation supported by board work or OHP.

Instructions

Advice given in activity 6.2b also applies here.
In planning for your part in the lesson you need to do the following:
- Carefully check the scheme of work for the topic and the depth of treatment required.
- Review any past examination questions that might be appropriate.
- Clarify why you are doing this part of the lesson in this way rather than any other. Write out a behavioural objective for the pupils' learning.
- Write out the key points of the explanation and order them in a logical sequence. Preface the sequence with an overview and a question that the explanation addresses.
- Find any audio-visual aids which may support your explanation.
- Estimate how long the explanation will take:
    10 to 15 minutes is enough for a motivated, above average group
    plan for shorter times with less motivated learners.
- Discuss the lesson plan with your team-teaching partner.

Before you take charge of the explanation you need to organize the following:

- Requisition audio-visual aids if appropriate.
- Check that the audio-visual aids are working.

During the time that you take charge of the explanation you need to do the following:

- Raise the problem that your explanation will address (see activity 6.2b).
- Give a brief overview of how the explanation is structured.
- Start at the first point and make it clearly.
- Return to the overview to show that you are moving onto the next point.
- Ask questions of the learners as you go along. Relate the questions to the learning objectives.
  Repeat the questions before you nominate a respondent.
  Spread the questions amongst groups: boys – girls, front – back and so on.
- Watch the clock.
  Stop the explanation if you are over-running and plan to continue in the next lesson.
- Summarize briefly.
- Return the class's attention to your team-teaching partner.

4.3 Planning, Organizing and Managing a Complete Lesson

Mentor's brief

Objective • Student teachers should be able to plan, organize and manage a complete lesson with adequate linkages between past lessons and future lessons within the scheme of work.

Time • Lesson time, and up to 2 hours, for the student teacher on each activity to be planned, discussed, organized, taught and reviewed
• Lesson time, and up to $\frac{1}{2}$ hour for the discussion of the plan, observation and debrief with mentor

Background

Experience has shown that student teachers who take charge of a complete lesson too early can be overtaken by the multitude of demands that are put upon them. They may revert to coping strategies that are recalled from their own experiences of learning. These may not always be the best strategies. Often it is chalk-and-talk with a transmission-mode of teaching and learning. Such strategies are certainly not well considered as they are often re-active rather than pro-active.

The starts and ends of lessons are the areas that will need special attention now. At the beginning of lessons, student teachers will have the entry phase of the lesson to deal with. The organizational and administrative aspects of coats, bags and the register will all need to be run through as smoothly as possible. Handing out books, reviewing homework, offering praise to those who have done well all need to be remembered and practised. The marshalling of pupils' recollections of past work needs to progress into the focusing on the next activities. At the end of lessons, student teachers must get into the habit of summarizing the learning of the lesson so as to re-focus pupils' ideas. Organizing homework, reminding people of disciplinary actions, if any have to be taken, rewarding those who have performed well and dismissing the class have to be worked at to achieve a flawless continuity. Concurrent observation, by student teachers, of other teachers achieving these actions, will help student teachers to improve their own performance. It is not wise, at this stage, to rely on memories of lessons observed several weeks ago.

Instructions

• Select the classes the student teacher will work with.
• Brief the student teacher on the scheme of work and the progress the pupils have made to date.
• Discuss the student teacher's preparation in advance of the lessons.

- Prepare for observation of the student teacher's work.
- Record data on the observation schedule.
- Debrief the student teacher.
- Set goals and targets for future lessons.
- Provide the student teacher with a copy of your written feedback.

Discussion points

- Handling arrivals:

   What directions were given on coats and bags?

   If arrivals are spaced over several minutes what work is there for the pupils when they arrive: copying board work, reading etc.?

   How are late arrivals dealt with? What are the school procedures and policies?

- Giving back marked work:

   Did the student teacher give out the books and thereby take the opportunity to become more familiar with who is who in the class?

   Did the student teacher pick out examples of good work and share with the class why it was good?

- Reviewing the work of the previous lesson:

   Was this done and were pupils' ideas elicited or was it a teacher review?

   Was it a well structured activity?

   Was the board used for keywords and concepts?

- Objectives:

   Are these written on the lesson plan? Are they written in terms of pupils' actions, knowledge and skills?

   Do activities lead to the achievement of the objectives?

- Focusing activities:

   Was a clear overview to this lesson provided?

- Varying activities:

   Is there sufficient variety of pupil activity in the lesson?

   Are activities appropriate to the pupils' skills and knowledge, concentration spans and interests.

   Is the variation well structured, e.g. quiet tasks at the beginning and ends of the lessons, or more open tasks later when pupils are less fresh?

- Timings for activities and watching the clock:

   Did the lesson end on time?

Was clearing away carried out before the end of the lesson?
Were pupils alerted to how much time is left for tasks?

- Summarizing:
    Was a summary provided?
    Was it clear, coherent and concise?
    Did it rely on ideas elicited from pupils?
    Was board work used to reinforce ideas?

- Giving homework:
    Was adequate time allowed for the pupils to copy it down.
    Was the homework relevant, achievable and clear?

- Sharing with the pupils what will be done in future lessons:
    Was there time for this?
    Was it linked to the scheme of work?

- Handling departures:
    Were disciplinary proceedings followed through with reminders?
    Was there quiet and calm before pupils left?

4.3 Planning, Organizing and Managing a Complete Lesson

Student Teacher's Brief

Many of the skills and strategies you have already rehearsed will be brought together, combined and refined in this activity

Objective

You should be able to plan, organize and manage a complete lesson, with adequate linkages between past lessons and future lessons, within the scheme of work.

Instructions

- Discuss the scheme of work with your mentor.
- Plan individual lessons.
- Use the notes below as a check-list.
- Start teaching the lessons.
- Modify your intentions, plans and actions in the light of feed-back from your mentor at de-briefing.

Notes on planning, organizing and managing complete lessons

Your planning should include the following:

- Formulating behavioural objectives for the pupils.
- Selecting appropriate learning activities.
- Checking for variety and appropriateness of activities.
- Planning extension activities for quicker pupils.
- Devising a linking strategy. Plan to review what happened in the previous lesson and to introduce this lesson.
- Checking the availability of equipment with the technicians.
- Formulating a summary for the end of the lesson.
- Devising homework for assessment and feedback.
- Writing out a complete lesson plan including what you will do, and more importantly what the pupils will do.

Your organizing should include the following:

- The requisitioning of apparatus in appropriate numbers for the groups whose sizes you have predetermined.
- The preparation, or ordering, of written resources, audio visual aids etc.
- The preparation of other materials, e.g. glue, scissors, crayons, large sheets of paper, etc.

In managing, you should pay attention to:

- The entry phase
- A revision and focusing phase
- Transitions between activities
- Clearing away
- Organizing of homework
- Consolidating and summarizing
- An orderly dismissal of the class.

4.4 Supplementing a Scheme of Work

Mentor's Brief

Objective • Student teachers should find, review and evaluate possible supplementary activities for part of a scheme of work.

Time • Several weeks of student teacher work between lessons
 • Two, 1 hour discussions with mentor

Background

When student teachers have confidence in managing complete lessons they need to be given the opportunity to review materials that can be used to supplement a scheme of work for a particular topic. They should be asked to carry out the review as a formal activity. They should draw upon the resources in the school, and at their college, to select supplementary activities.

Student teachers will have referred to schemes of work in previous lesson planning activities. Now is the time to stand back from the pressure of individual lesson plans and lessons to take a broader view of the progress of learners. This is an attempt to provide links between the general aims of programmes of study, schemes of work and the detail of lesson planning. The difference in detail of a lesson plan, scheme of work and programme of study need to be clarified so that the work can proceed at the right level. Generally speaking, *programmes of study* are concerned with broad-brush stroke pictures that will have aims and general areas of knowledge and skills sketched out. They will span a whole key-stage at a time. A *scheme of work* will repeat the aims of the programme of study and provide a schedule of termly, weekly and even lesson-by-lesson topics, activities and the objectives that the activities are designed to meet. The *lesson plan* is the document that student teachers should now be most familiar with. These operate at the level of the lesson and have an internal detailing of the structure of the lesson.

Instructions

- Identify a scheme of work that needs revising.
- Discuss the current scheme of work with the student teacher.
- Direct the student teacher to sources of supplementary materials at the school. Suggest they find supplementary materials in their college.
- Set a deadline for the receipt of a written report.
- Review the report with the student teacher.

4.4 Supplementing a Scheme of Work

Student Teacher's Brief

This activity is intended to help both you and the rest of the science department. Schemes of work need updating in a systematic manner. You can contribute to the work of the science department by carrying out one such review. You will need to draw upon the knowledge and skills you have developed through activities in other chapters in this book.

Objective

Student teachers should find, review and evaluate possible supplementary activities for part of a scheme of work.

Instructions

- Your mentor will provide you with a topic that could usefully be reviewed.
- Obtain a copy of the scheme of work for the topic.
- Arrange to have access to the materials used to support learning of the topic.
- Use the following questions as a guide to a formal review of the scheme of work:

     Are the aims clearly expressed? Are they reflected in appropriate activities?

     Have the aims been translated into achievable objectives for the pupils? Do the activities match the objectives?

     Is there an appropriate range of types of activities? How might that range be different?

     What provision is there made for language development in the activities? Are learners with special language needs catered for? How?

     Is there a good spread of activities that reflect the processes of science? Could this be improved?

     Is any particular view of science dominant in the activities? Is this a consistent view or not?

     What provision is made for pupils with different levels of performance through the provision of differentiated activities?

     How well does the assessment match the expressed objectives?

     Is the performance of pupils on assessment tasks mapped onto Science in the National Curriculum? How might this mapping be improved?

- Sift and sort through resources in the school and at your college to find alternative activities for pupils. The emphasis at this stage is on improving variety and appropriateness and not on whether they can be fitted into the time schedule.
- Write a report on alternative activities for pupils that might be used to supplement the scheme of work. Justify your choices.
- Discuss the report with your mentor.

4.5 Revising and Trialling Part of a Scheme of Work

Mentor's Brief

Objective • Student teachers should produce a revision of part of a scheme of work that they have trialled in their own teaching.

Time • Several weeks of student teacher work between lessons
• Two, 1 hour discussions with mentor

Instructions

Following on directly from activity 4.4 this work aims to extend the student teacher's professional growth with the compilation of a revised scheme of work.

• Ask the student teacher to return to the report they produced in activity 4.4. and to select from the supplementary materials they have gathered suitable activities that might be used in the scheme of work.
• Preview the revised scheme with the student teacher.
• Set a deadline for receipt of the final version of the revised scheme of work.
• Collect the final version.
• Discuss the report with the student teacher.

4.5 Revising and Trialling Part of a Scheme of Work

Student Teacher's Brief

Objective

You should produce a revision of part of a scheme of work that you have trialled in your own teaching.

Instructions

The work you are to revise here is for a series of about six lessons, say three week's work with pupils, no more.

• From the work carried out in activity 4.4 you should now have a comprehensive view of the scheme of work on the topic as carried out in your school, together with notes on comments on supplementary activities.

- Use your knowledge, skills and resources to provide an improved scheme of work. You will need to do the following:

    Use the resources in your college library and science area to find as many activities as you can that relate to the topic. Include computer assisted learning, videos, worksheets, slides and pre-recorded audio-tapes. Find SATIS activities that may be relevant and look through established schemes published as textbooks (see activities 8.3 and 8.5).

    Review these resources and activities.

    Look through Science in the National Curriculum, at the appropriate key stage, to find what might be statutorily required.

    Sketch out different pathways through the topic in terms of sub-topics – that is what should be taught first what should be taught next, and so on. Try to find at least two different starting points, end points and pathways.

    Review your pathways through the sub-topics for their suitability for the pupils, resources and ways of working in your school.

    Start to map your selected pathway through the sub-topics onto a schedule of lessons in a scheme of work.

    Relocate sub-topics whilst you add activities and behavioural objectives.

    Review the scheme of work and again relocate and revise sub-topics, activities and objectives.

    Map Science in the National Curriculum levels onto activities where appropriate.

    Add suitable assessments at suitable places. For this you will have to refer back to the original sheets that should accompany programmes of study in your science department.

    Review the scheme of work.

- Present your draft scheme to your mentor.
- Revise the scheme in the light of your mentor's comments.
- Trial the scheme of work through teaching the activities in your lessons.
- Evaluate the lessons and revise the scheme of work.
- Present the final version to your mentor for discussion.

Chapter 5

Science Investigations

Aims

The aims of this chapter are to help student teachers to:

- become more familiar with the variety of learning opportunities offered by investigational work in science;
- develop skills and strategies for helping pupils to learn in open situations;
- gain knowledge and skills in analysing investigations so as to plan for progression and differentiation within a topic;
- plan strategies for formative assessment of pupils doing investigations in topics.

Introduction

Say 'science lesson' to most people and they would probably think of something involving 'practical work'. However, as the years have gone by since the major curriculum revisions of the 1960s and 1970s, the nature and value of 'practical work' have been examined and questioned. Current curriculum innovation focuses more on explorations and investigations. These are not synonyms, the change of word is important and indicates a more thoughtful approach to science education. In science education, pupils build knowledge; they build knowledge about the content of science and about the way in which science is done. In doing this, they invariably practice the processes of science (see also Chapter 7). This chapter concentrates on the teacher's role in setting up, managing and assessing the type of work in science called investigations. By investigations we mean any activity in which pupils use the processes of science to build knowledge which is new to them.

Investigations offer pupils an opportunity to be involved in the processes of doing science for themselves: to combine their theoretical knowledge and understanding of science with their practical knowledge and skills. Simon *et al.* (1992) identified three phases in investigatory work: defining the problem, choosing a method and arriving at solutions. Aspects of investigatory work can be categorized as being on a spectrum of openness. An understanding of this idea helps teachers to match investigations to individuals and to groups, to plan for progression in their teaching and to structure their assessment of a pupil's attainment.

Pupils in Year 1 are perfectly capable of carrying out open-ended investigations. However, their thoughts, actions and products will be different from those of pupils in Year 11. Gradual development of skills and knowledge changes the qualitative nature of pupils approaches to investigations. The descriptions at the ten levels for Sc1 are best interpreted as an attempt to provide guidance on the qualitative changes that take place as pupils progress in their investigatory skills. Qualitative changes in pupils' knowledge and skills are not to be confused with the openness that teachers build into investigatory work. How a pupil performs, in terms of attainment, depends upon the pupil. Providing openness in investigatory tasks is, by and large, a planning, organization and management problem and thus depends on the teacher.

In activity 5.1, investigations which differ in their openness are examined and the possible learning opportunities in open tasks are explored. In activity 5.2, a variety of techniques for helping pupils to learn in open situations are introduced. These techniques can be practised by student teachers with small groups of pupils within a lesson taken by another teacher, or within their own lessons. In activity 5.3, the focus moves to planning a whole lesson in such a way that a structure for learning is provided within an open situation. The fourth section deals with issues of planning for progression and differentiation. The final section deals with assessment issues in investigations, in particular planning to maximize formative assessment opportunities through pupils taking an active part in the assessment process.

5.1a Analysing Investigations for Openness

Mentor's Brief

Objectives • Student teachers should be able to apply the idea of openness in investigations to analyse activities for pupils in the school's programme of study.

Time • 1 hour for student teachers to read notes and analyse worksheets for investigatory work
• $\frac{1}{2}$ hour discussion with mentor

Instructions

• Ask the student teacher to read the notes about investigations and to discuss their ideas about openness with you afterwards.

- Select two practical activities used at your school and ask the student teacher to analyse them for openness.
- Discuss the student teacher's analysis and their suggestions for modifications.

Summary

The discussion at the end of activity 5.1a should emphasize that investigations may have different degrees of openness. Making something more open does not necessarily make it easier or harder, it just makes it different. The type and the amount of difference are important and can be helpful in planning, managing and assessing the investigation.

5.1a   Analysing Investigations for Openness

Student Teacher's Brief

In order to build knowledge, scientists investigate the world. To investigate natural phenomena, pupils use various processes of science. In using these processes, pupils pass through three phases of an investigation:

- Defining the problem
- Choosing a method
- Arriving at solutions.

Each of these phases can be analysed in terms of their openness. An understanding of the concept of openness allows you to plan, manage and assess investigatory work more effectively. The notes that follow give advice on how more openness may be introduced into pupils' investigations at each of these phases.

Objective

You should be able to apply the idea of openness in investigations to analyse activities for pupils in your school's programme of study.

Instructions

- Read the notes below about investigations and about openness.
- Read the analysis of the two sets of investigations given after the notes.
- Discuss your understanding of openness with your mentor.
- Analyse the practical activities in your school's schemes of work

---

selected by your mentor. Decide what it is specifically about each investigation that could make it more open or more closed? Decide how the investigations could be made more open and what the consequences might be for pupils?

- Discuss this analysis with your mentor.

Notes about openness

Making an investigation more closed may make it either easier or more difficult: easier, by requiring pupils to think less (see set 1 of the investigations below), or more difficult, when it constrains pupils to ideas and techniques with which they cannot operate (see set 2). Open investigations can be interpreted in a variety of different ways by pupils, and how they interpret them will also affect the difficulty of the investigation.

Investigations: Set 1
1a) Copper sulphate solution conducts electricity. Investigate how the flow of electricity through the solution is affected by the concentration of the copper sulphate solution. Set up a circuit as shown in the diagram using 100 cm^3 of copper sulphate solution in a 250 cm^3 beaker and an ammeter to measure the current. You are provided with four different concentrations of copper sulphate (0.01M, 0.05M, 0.1M, 0.5M), which you should test in turn.
1b) Copper sulphate solution conducts electricity. Investigate how the flow of electricity through the solution is affected by the concentration of the copper sulphate solution.
1c) Copper sulphate solution conducts electricity. Find out the factors that affect the flow of electricity through a solution of copper sulphate.

Investigations: Set 2
2a) The kinetic theory predicts that as the temperature of a solution is increased the ions will move more rapidly. How do you expect temperature to affect the flow of electricity through an ionic solution? Carry out an investigation to test your ideas.
2b) Investigate the effect of temperature on the rate of flow of current through an ionic solution.
2c) Investigate the factors that affect the flow of electricity through solutions of salts.

Degrees of openness

The degree of openness of an investigation can be represented as a position on a spectrum. One might consider three spectra; one for each phase of investigatory work.

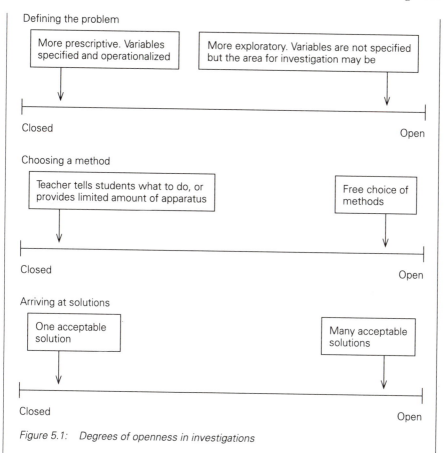

Figure 5.1:   *Degrees of openness in investigations*

Defining the problem
In defining the problem, the openness depends on the level of prescription in the statement of the investigation. All the investigations given above are about the flow of electricity through ionic solutions, but the factors to be investigated are stated at different levels of specificity. For example, in investigation 1a the independent variable (concentration of copper sulphate) is specified, and the dependent variable (flow of current) is measured using an ammeter. Some of the control variables are also specified (i.e. the volume of solution and the type of electrodes) but others are left unspecified. For this investigation, most variables are therefore specified and some help is given in operationalizing them, i.e. deciding how to measure or to control them when doing the investigation. This investigation lies towards the closed end of the spectrum. By contrast the variables to be investigated are not even specified in investigations 1c and 2c which both lie towards the open end of the spectrum.

Choosing a method

In a more open investigation, pupils have more choice of method, whereas in a more closed investigation the teacher either tells the pupil what to do or gives such a limited amount of apparatus that the effect is the same. Another factor that can influence the variety of methods that are used is the position of the investigation in relation to other work. If the pupils have recently carried out some experimental work using electro-chemical cells, then the methods may already be defined to some degree. Some teachers have found that existing tasks which are relatively closed can be opened up by giving pupils a choice of methods. The investigations in the two sets above are open to some extent in that the pupils have to make some choices about how to carry out each investigation.

Arriving at solutions

When considering openness, in terms of solutions to a problem, open investigations have many acceptable solutions. An acceptable solution is one that is consistent with the way in which the investigation has been defined and operationalized. For example, in investigation 1c, pupils may reach a number of different solutions depending on which factors they investigated and how they carried out their investigations. When investigations are very open there are opportunities to match investigations with pupils' abilities and progress. Investigation 2c could be interpreted as a comparison between two solutions taken off the shelf in the laboratory. The pupils may be interested in discovering whether one solution conducts better than the other, as indicated by the brightness of a light bulb for example. Other pupils may carry out quantitative investigations of variables related to their knowledge and understanding of ions in solutions, and may even try to develop a mathematical model of their findings.

Not all investigations need have similar degrees of openness. The amount of openness appropriate for a particular investigation will depend on the pupils' past experiences and present needs, and on the aims of a particular lesson. Investigation 2a has been made more closed by linking it to ideas of ionic theory, whereas investigation 2c does not necessarily carry that conceptual demand. Investigation 1a is made closed by specifying and operationalizing the variables to be investigated, whereas investigation 2c offers more opportunities for the pupils to formulate their own questions and methods of investigation.

5.1b Aims of Investigations

Mentor's Brief

Objective • Student teachers should be able to report on a range of opinions, both pupils' and science teachers, on why pupils do investigations in science lessons.

Time • 3 hours total for student teacher to talk with science teachers and pupils as well as to write a brief report
       • ½ hour discussion with mentor

Background

When asked why they included 'open-ended' work in their curriculum (Simon *et al.*, 1992, Chapter 2), most teachers gave affective reasons, such as to give the initiative to students, to motivate them and to encourage enjoyment. A much smaller number emphasized developing skills and processes, and fewer than 10 per cent emphasized conceptual development. Lack of clarity in the aims, and in particular the low emphasis on developing knowledge, cognitive and manipulative skills and processes were identified as major weaknesses in many lessons involving investigations.

Instructions

• The student teacher will need to talk members of the science department about the aims of investigations.
• He or she will also need to talk with some pupils about their ideas on why there are investigations in their science course.
• Ask the student teacher to write a brief report on his or her findings.
• Discuss the student teacher's findings with him or her.

Discussion points

Pupils' responses are likely to be related to particular investigations that they remember. Only exceptional pupils will have the overview that the teacher has, and therefore rarely do pupils think about general features of investigations. The average pupil's strategies are ones of remarking on the 'trees' rather than seeing the 'wood'.

When asked about what they are learning in investigation 1c (in activity 5.1a) many pupils will say that it is to find out what factors affect the conductivity of copper sulphate solution. Whilst this is the purpose of the investigation, it is not the purpose of the learning activity: its purpose may be in the skills and processes of setting up an investigation. The pupils will not see the educational purpose of the investigation unless this is made clear to them. It is therefore important that student teachers are clear on the purpose of a learning activity involving an investigation and that they communicate this to the pupils.

5.1b Aims of Investigations

Student Teacher's Brief

Objective

You should be able to report on a range of opinions, both pupils' and science teachers', on why pupils do investigations in science lessons.

Instructions

- Talk to members of the science department about reasons for doing investigations. Note down what they say.
  Analyse the frequency of their responses for the categories outlined below:
    - To gain knowledge and understanding by exploring phenomena through scientific investigations.
    - To give students insight into how scientific knowledge is created.
    - To use existing knowledge to raise questions and formulate investigations.
    - To develop practical skills and systematic procedures for carrying out investigations.
    - To use initiative to make decisions.
    - To provide motivation and enjoyment.
    - Other.
- Observe a lesson during which pupils are carrying out an investigation.
  Whilst they are carrying out the investigation, ask some of them what they think they are learning through doing the investigation.
  Do the pupils have the same perceptions about the aims of the activity as the teacher?
- Write a brief report on your findings. In your report consider the following:
    - What are the main reasons for doing investigations in your school?
    - Do you agree with this emphasis?
    - Are there any learning outcomes that you think are underemphasized?
    - What do pupils think they are learning in investigations?
    - Reflexively, how much has this activity of surveying opinions on aims of investigations been an open investigation?
- Discuss your report with your mentor.

5.2 Techniques for Guiding Pupils in Open Investigations

Mentor's Brief

Objective • Student teachers should be able to use two different techniques for helping pupils with their investigations.

Time • 2 hours planning, team-teaching and writing a brief report
  • $\frac{1}{2}$ hour discussion with the class teacher and mentor

Background

The techniques suggested here provide ways of making public, and sharing, pupils' perceptions of their investigatory work. This will allow the teacher to probe why pupils are choosing to proceed in particular ways. This helps pupils think about their own thinking. The techniques are drawn form the work of the OPENS project (Simon, 1992) which looked critically at teachers' strategies for developing pupils' investigations.

Instructions

- Direct the student teacher to lessons where investigatory work will be carried out in the near future. Brief colleagues as appropriate.
- Direct the student teacher to the notes on techniques for guiding pupils in investigations.
- Arrange to discuss the lessons and the student teacher's brief report with the class teacher.

Discussion points

Using techniques to guide pupils in open-ended investigations is not the same as making the investigation more closed. Useful guiding techniques will focus the pupils' attention on the processes they must pursue and thereby provide them with structured help in those processes. This is not the same as telling the pupils the answer.

Asking pupils if they have planned a fair test is not the same as telling them which variable to control. Similarly asking pupils if they have considered how to record their data is not the same as telling them which table to use for their results and asking pupils if they have linked their conclusions to their results is not showing them how to carry out an analysis. What each of these have in common is the deliberate attempt to refer pupils to the processes of science so as to help them become more aware of how they operate those processes. These processes will need earlier illustration in other less open practical activities where teachers refer to what is happening in terms of scientific method.

5.2 Techniques for Guiding Pupils in Open Investigations

Student Teacher's Brief

This activity gives you an opportunity to use two different techniques for helping pupils with their investigations. The activity is designed to be carried out as part of a lesson you are team-teaching with another

---

teacher. You will have to do some preliminary planning with the class's teacher.

Instructions

- Discuss with your mentor in which lessons you might team-teach investigatory work.
- Read the notes below on techniques for helping pupils in investigations.
- Discuss with the class's teacher how you might collaborate in team-teaching.
- Prepare your part of the lesson.
- Team-teach the lesson.
- Write a brief summary report.
- Discuss the report with the class teacher and your mentor.

Notes on techniques for guiding pupils in investigations

The techniques suggested below are designed to help pupils to carry out their own investigations. The main idea is to provide a structure to help pupils to work in an open situation without telling them what to do. The techniques focus on

- using a thinking schedule with pupils
- using variables tables.

Technique 1: Using a thinking schedule with pupils
The schedule below is designed to elicit how the pupils are going about doing the investigation. It can be given to the pupils at the beginning of the investigation. It does not tell pupils what to do, but provides the teacher with information about how they are tackling the investigation. As the teacher circulates around the class during the investigation, the responses to the thinking schedule provide a focus for discussion between the teacher and the pupils.

Thinking schedule for pupils

1. My question about _____ is / What I am going to find out is
2. What I already know about this
3. What I think will happen is
4. I think this will happen because
5. The equipment I need is (draw the equipment if you want to)
6. Do I need to make a fair-test?
7. Why I need to make a fair-test
8. I will make my test fair by

9. What happened during my experiment?
10. Is it different from what I thought would happen?
11. What have I found that I did not know before?

Defining the problem
It is important to clarify what investigation the pupils are actually carrying out, and what skills, processes, knowledge and understanding they bring to their investigations. Pupils often reformulate investigations in ways which are different from how the teacher intended but which nevertheless still provide valuable learning experiences.

Use the pupils' responses to 1–4 to clarify how the pupils have understood the investigation. Try to establish what variables they consider to be important, how they are going to control or measure them, and why they are planning the investigation in this way. Pupils often have an expectation of what will happen when they carry out their investigation. Pupils' expectations also determine what they observe and how they undertake the activity. Asking the pupils what they think will happen and why, will encourage them to focus on predictions and may also help them to hypothesize.

Choosing a method
Use the answers to points 5–8 to focus on whether appropriate procedures such as 'fair-testing' are being used. Explore whether the pupils have identified the important variables to control. They should be able to justify why some factors need to be controlled and others not. Often when pupils try to put their plans into action they need to modify them in response to their trials. Find out in what ways the pupils think their techniques are inadequate and what could be done to improve them. Check that what they are doing enables them to answer the questions that the investigation is about. Ask them whether they think it does.

Finding solutions
Thinking about what they have done and why helps pupils to become more aware of the processes that they have gone through in the investigation. It also helps them to develop systematic procedures that can be applied to other investigations and reinforces their conceptual learning. Use the responses to points 9–11 to find out what pupils have learnt about strategies for investigation and how they could improve their experimental design. Find out what new knowledge and understanding they have gained.

Technique 2: Using variables tables
Another simple technique for gaining insight into pupils' understanding of the investigation is to use a pupil-designed variables table. Pupils are given a blank table without any headings. The table can be introduced in a whole class discussion about the variables involved in the

investigation. Pupils are asked to identify the key variables relevant to their investigation and to write a list of these. The pupils can then choose one variable as the *independent* variable; identify the variable that they will measure, the *dependent* variable; and place this in the last column of the table. All the other variables that might affect the *dependent* variable are placed as headings to the other columns. An example of a variables table for the following investigation is shown.

This table is taken from investigatory work into whether copper sulphate solution conducts electricity. Pupils were asked to complete a table to show how they would systematically change the factors they thought might affect the flow of electricity through a solution of copper sulphate.

Table 5.1: A partially completed variable table

Concentration of copper sulphate solution	Temperature of solution (°C)	Depth of electrodes (mm)	Flow of electricity
0.1 M	20	4	
0.08M	20	4	
0.04M	40	4	
0.01M	40	4	

The table shows that the pupils are changing two variables at the same time (the *independent* variables) and this makes it impossible to know whether the concentration or temperature are having an effect. It also shows what the pupils think are the important variables to control: the depth of the electrodes has been controlled, but from this table it doesn't seem as if the distance between electrodes has been controlled. Tables such as this aid pupils in planning their investigation by focusing their attention on the systematic control of variables through the simple expedient of being systematic in quantifying them. The tables also make the pupils' thinking more obvious to the teacher.

Either ask the teacher who is running the lesson to introduce the variables table to pupils in the introduction to the lesson, or work with small groups getting them to draw up their own. Use the table as a focus for identifying key variables and how they are to be measured or controlled in the investigation.

5.3 Structuring Investigation Lessons

Mentor's Brief

Objective • Student teachers should be able to plan, organize and manage lessons with structured sequences of activities for pupils' investigations.

Time   • Several hours for the student teacher to read the notes, plan an investigation and trial it with a class
         • $\frac{1}{2}$ hour discussion with mentor

Background

Allowing pupils a totally free hand for their investigations courts disaster. The main emphasis of this section is that pupils need a series of structured activities by which they can advance their investigation. Substantial amounts of time need to be devoted to teacher-organized thinking, discussion and writing. Practical activity is only one part of the whole. To promote that thinking and discussion, student teachers need to plan investigation lessons involving pupil activities such as whole class and small group discussion, writing and reading.

Instructions

   • Instruct the student teacher to read the notes in activity 5.3.
   • Select a suitable lesson in which the student teacher can try out the investigation structure.
   • The student teacher plans the lesson.
   • Discuss it before the student teacher carries it out.
   • Observe the lesson. Keep a note of the time spent on different parts of the lesson and the main focus of pupil discussions.
   • Discuss the lesson with the student teacher.

Discussion points

Alternative strategies for getting pupils to discuss ideas at the beginning and end of lessons might include the following:

   • At the beginning of the lesson:
         Use of thinking schedules and variables tables (activity 5.2).
         Brainstorming in groups of five or six.
         Not allowing pupils to start practical work until they have selected apparatus and can explain how they will use it.
         Planning in one lesson and carrying out the plan in the next.
   • At the end of the lesson:
         Class discussion of posters of findings.
         Use of thinking schedules, and discussion in small groups (activity 5.2).

5.3 Structuring Investigation Lessons

Student Teacher's Brief

The three phases of an investigation, defining a problem, choosing a method and finding solutions, must be realized in the classroom through

---

science teachers planning appropriate activities for pupils that will take them through the three phases. This might occur in one lesson but it is more likely that the work will extend across several lessons.

Objective

You should be able to plan, organize and manage lessons with structured sequences of pupil activities for investigations.

Instructions

- Read the notes and case-study below.
- Use the lesson structure outlined in the notes for investigations to plan a lesson or short series of lessons involving an investigation.
- Teach the lesson/s.
- Discuss the lesson/s with your mentor.

Notes on structuring investigation lessons

The lesson structure below is designed to involve pupils in actively thinking about what they are doing. It is designed to promote engagement of pupils' knowledge, their cognitive and manipulative skills and their investigative strategies. A lesson structure that aims to promote active mental engagement in investigations should motivate pupils, provide periods of time when pupils think about strategies being used in the investigation and give them time to reflect on what they have learnt. A useful structure consists of five activities for pupils you will notice that only a small part of the time may be spent in practical work:

- focusing — thinking about a demonstration and discussing ideas
- exploring — discussing, writing and doing a practical
- reporting — discussing and writing
- consolidating — discussing
- applying — doing practical, writing or discussing

Case-study: Investigation of Suitable Materials for a Lab-coat

Year 10 pupils
Teachers and pupils were generally not familiar with investigations, but had done a preparatory lesson on fair testing. The aim of the investigation was to develop pupils' ideas of fair-testing.

Focusing activities

The investigation was introduced towards the end of a topic on materials. The teacher came into the laboratory in an old lab-coat with holes and stains in it. She led a class discussion about the purposes of a lab-coat and then organized the pupils into groups of about four or five to make a list of all the features that they thought were important in a lab-coat. She collected the ideas of the pupils on the board and then introduced the pupils to the investigation: which of the materials provided was the best for a lab-coat? The pupils then had to identify the factors that were related to the problem and to choose the one that they thought was most important to investigate.

Exploring activities

The pupils were helped to reformulate some of their ideas into appropriate investigations. Some investigated the flammability of materials, others chemical resistance and others strength. They planned how they would carry out a fair test, made some initial trials and then made a more detailed plan which they carried out the next lesson. Next lesson the large groups divided into two to carry out their investigations.

Reporting activities

After the pupils had recorded their results, each group was asked to report what they had found out and how they had carried out the investigation. The conclusions were tabulated on the board. Different groups had reached different conclusions and the pupils were encouraged to discuss one another's conclusions with respect to both the strategies used in the investigations and the function of the material in a lab-coat. This led into the consolidating phase.

Consolidating activities

The discussion focused on the main aim of the lesson: fair testing. In order to make decisions about fair testing, pupils had to draw on concepts such as the effect of surface area or concentration on rate of reaction. After the discussion, the pupils were asked to complete their thinking schedules.

Applying stage

The teacher drew on the ideas developed about fair-testing in later topics and used the ideas about rates of reactions when introducing a topic about rates later in the year. An alternative strategy could have been to set a homework which required pupils to apply the ideas from this investigation in a different context.

5.4 Pupils' development of Investigational Skills

Mentor's Brief

Objectives	• Student teachers should be able to interpret and apply criteria for different levels of pupil development in investigations.
Time	• 3 hours for the student teacher to read the investigations and compile a report
	• 1 hour discussion with mentor

Background

The descriptions of the ten levels of development for investigational skills in Science in the National Curriculum require interpretation for personal application. It is not immediately obvious what a given level of performance would look like when translated into the context of a particular investigation: it requires experience and judgment to carry out the translation. Student teachers can be helped to develop that experience and judgment by going through a sifting and sorting exercise so as to compare their intuitive judgments against the descriptions given in Science in the National Curriculum. Through this experience of looking for similarities and differences, student teachers can then tune their judgments to the levels of development in Science in the National Curriculum.

Instructions

- Provide the student teacher with copies of the investigations of at least one class of pupils. It will be useful to have more than one investigation across different years if possible, ideally Year 7 and Year 11, so as to see progression between cohorts as well as differentiation within a cohort.
- Ask the student teacher to write a brief report on the variation in the pupils' investigations using the level descriptions for ScI as a guide.
- Discuss the report with the student teacher.

Discussion points

To carry out investigations, pupils will need to use their knowledge and cognitive processes. These develop and change as pupils have more and wider experience in science education, i.e., there is progression. Performance on any one investigation requires a combination of content knowledge and process skills. This intimate mix of content and process makes the estimation of any one pupil's level of development from a single investigation of dubious reliability. A more reliable assessment of any one pupil's level of development can be obtained by looking at a pupil's performance across several investigations.

5.4 Pupils' Development of Investigational Skills

Student Teacher's Brief

Pupils make progress in their knowledge and cognitive skills during the time of their compulsory schooling: the product of a Year 7 pupil will not be the same as that of a pupil in Year 11. In investigatory work in science there is progress in pupils' performances and this progress can be characterized in different ways. The ten level scale of the National Curriculum is one way of attempting to characterize this pupil progress.

Objective

You should be able to interpret and apply criteria for different levels of pupils' development in investigations.

Instructions

- Collect together pupils' reports on their investigations that are provided by your mentor. Take them to a room where you can spread them out on a bench.
- Sift through the reports and see what differences you notice. This is a matter of looking for differentiated outcomes. Look for qualitatively different features. Write descriptions of these features in the pupils' investigations.
- Consider your descriptions and decide if they can be rationalized into a simpler scheme that reflects some progression in pupils' investigational skills. Rearrange your descriptions into a simpler scheme if possible.
- Sift and sort through the reports again. For one of the descriptions arrange the pupils' reports on a bench in order of progression. Sample adjacent reports and move them to other places in the sequence if you change your judgment. Make a note of the final order you settle on.
- Turn to the descriptions of the ten levels of development for investigations in Science in the National Curriculum. Find descriptions that reflect your current concern. Read through them carefully.
- Return to the pupils' investigation reports laid out on the bench. Use the descriptions of the levels of development from Science in the National Curriculum to relocate the pupils' investigations into a sequence that reflects the progression in the levels of development. Note down this order.
- Compare the first ordering of pupils' investigations, according

to the qualitative differences that you first noticed, with the order produced in considering the levels of development in Science in the National Curriculum. Find the work of pupils that occupy different places in the two sequences. Re-read the pupils' work and reconsider your judgment. Make a note of why there was a difference.

- Repeat this exercise with other qualitative differences that you first noticed.
- Write a brief report on assessing the level of development of a pupil's investigation.
- Discuss your report with your mentor.

5.5 Raising Pupil Performance on Investigations

Mentor's Brief

Objective   •   Student teachers should be able to use the technique of shared marking standards with pupils so as to raise the level of their performance on investigations.

Time   •   4 hours for student teacher marking pupils' investigations, writing annotated version of the investigation and working with the class
   •   1 hour discussion with mentor

Background

Pupils can improve their performance when they know what they are expected to achieve. In the whirl of practical activity and investigations, student teachers can sometimes fail to articulate publicly what they think privately and the pupils are left to guess. This activity is intended to provide the student teacher with a pupil activity that publicly rehearses the standards to be attained. This concern is paralleled in other activities: activity 9.4, on cognitive development, and 9.5, on differentiation, are concerned with raising levels of pupils' performance. Activity 10.4, which encourages pupils to write their own questions, involves sharing assessment criteria and judgments with pupils.

Instructions

- Discuss with the student teacher which class and which investigation would be appropriate for this activity.
- Review the student teacher's lesson preparation and annotated account of the investigation before the lesson.

- Team-teach the feedback activity with the student teacher taking the lead role.
- Discuss the lesson with the student teacher.

Discussion points

Reliability of marking will be one of the issues which is likely to emerge with the pupils. This is difficult for pupils to grasp and they may need reassurance from you in order to accept that uncertainty in assessment is natural and not just the 'fault' of an inexperienced student teacher. With the student teacher, decide what should be done to build upon this work.

5.5 Raising Pupil Performance on Investigations

Student Teacher's Brief

Marks or grades given on performance provide pupils with an indication of how well they are doing with respect to the standards set by the assessor or marker. However, the marker's standards are not automatically transferred to the pupil upon receipt of their marks. The pupils only know that they have not reached the maximum level expected. The pupils also need to know what the maximum level looks like in terms of their expected behaviour and output. To transfer this knowledge to the pupils requires a deliberate sharing of standards between pupils and teacher. One way of achieving this is to get the pupils to mark their own work so they can compare the marks they would have given themselves with the marks the teacher gives them.

Objective

You should be able to use the technique of sharing marking standards with pupils so as to raise the level of their performance on investigations.

Instructions

- Discuss with your mentor the best time to work with pupils who have just done and written up an investigation.
- Mark their work but keep separate notes of your decisions; do not write on the pupils' books.
- Write your own account of the investigation and add some comments about the marking.

The worksheet for pupils, 'Heating saucepan investigation' shown below, was written by adapting the written account of one pupil to bring

---

out some key points in order to take other pupils a little further in their investigating. For example, the two values of temperature were adjusted to be slightly different so as to give an opportunity to discuss the significance of small differences and the necessity to repeat readings in order to check on reliability.

- Before giving back the pupils' accounts, give out your own account and discuss the marking with the pupils. With the example shown below, the pupils had their own version of the national curriculum and were able to check the marking decisions against what their version said.
- Return the pupils' accounts and ask them to mark their own work in the same way. You could ask them to do this in pairs and to check their decisions with each other.
- When they have done this, you may tell the pupils the mark or level which you gave to their work; indeed, the pupils will probably ask for it. There will be some differences of opinion and these provide the key learning experience for the pupils as they re-adjust their perceptions of what it is they must do to achieve a good mark.
- Discuss your experiences with your mentor.

Some of the differences in marking can be accounted for by explaining that you took into account not only what the pupils had written but also what you saw them do and heard them say as they were doing the investigation. This can be rewarding for those who worked well but did not manage to put it all down on paper. It can be a salutary lesson for those who messed about or copied from their partner during the investigation, particularly if you had occasion to speak to them about it at the time. You can remind them of this when you tell them the mark or level you have given them.

You should explain to the pupils that the mark which will be used for reporting purposes at the end of the year will be arrived at by a consideration of all the investigations which they have done. This provides an opportunity to deal with some issues of reliability. The pupils will know that they do better on some occasions than on others and most of them will accept the need to use the results of several investigations in order to smooth out their fluctuations in performance.

It will be too time-consuming to do this kind of analysis with every investigation the pupils do, but you should do it at least twice in a term and you should encourage the pupils to do it for themselves at other times. You should explain to the pupils that they should always look at ways of improving their own work. When they do their next investigation, remind them of what they did last time and tell them to do it again.

Heating Saucepan Investigation

The Investigation

The problem

Will water boil in a container at a higher temperature with the lid on than with the lid off?

Hypothesis

I think the water will boil at a higher temperature with the lid on because the lid will prevent loss of heat by convection.

Plan

Use two beakers which are the same.
Put the same amount of water in each.
Put a lid on one beaker, boil the water and take the temperature.
Leave the lid off the other beaker, use the same Bunsen flame, boil the water and take the temperature.

Apparatus needed

2 beakers	Tripod
Thermometer	Wire gauze
Bunsen burner	Heat-proof mat
Cardboard to make lid for beaker	
Eye goggles	

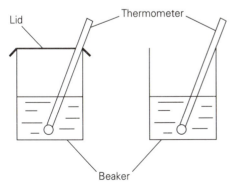

The investigation

I did the investigation as described in the plan. I made a hole in the cardboard lid so that I

Comments

PLANNING

The problem is posed in the form of a question. At the end I should be able to see my answer to the question.

Hypothesis: I can say what might happen and give a scientific reason. (Level 5) If I did not give a reason, it would be a prediction, not a hypothesis. Not enough in this investigation to make it Level 6.

Plan: Using the same beakers, same amount of water and same Bunsen flame makes any comparison between the beakers fair. (Level 5)

Apparatus chosen. (Provided the apparatus is used properly and accurate readings taken, this will be Level 5)

PERFORMING

More information is needed about how the same amount of

The Investigation
(cont.)

could put the thermometer in. I let the water boil for about 1 minute before taking the temperature.

The results were:

	Temperature
With lid	99.5°C
Without lid	99.0°C

Conclusions

I think there is no real difference in the readings, therefore the temperature is not higher with the lid on.

If there is a difference, it seems to be very small so I should have taken more readings over a longer period of time.

I have since found out that the temperature of boiling water will increase if the pressure increases — as in a pressure cooker. The lid on the beaker did not keep the steam in and so the pressure did not increase. The lid on a real saucepan might be heavy and a better fit so the temperature might be higher with the lid on.

Comments
(cont.)

water was measured, what size beakers were used, and how much water was put in them. This is about Level 4 at the moment.

Used the apparatus correctly (Level 4) and made accurate readings (Level 5/6).

INTERPRETING AND EVALUATING

The conclusion links the results to the original question. (Level 4)

There is a good evaluation of the investigation. A suggestion is made about how to improve the investigation.

There is a link to other science, i.e. pressure and temperature. (Level 6)

Chapter 6

Communicating Science

Aim

Learning science involves learning the languages of science. Scientists listen to each other, speak, read and write to each other. They also communicate ideas in pictorial and diagrammatic form, tables and graphs. It is easy to appreciate that a language of words has a grammar and vocabulary and that specialist fields, like science, have ways of using language that are peculiar to themselves. It is less obvious that there is a vocabulary and grammar of graphs and drawings. One has to learn to 'read', as well as learn how to 'write', drawings and graphs. This is particularly true in some branches of science with their idiosyncratic diagrammatic conventions. Student teachers can forget this and may see drawings as being self-explanatory. After all we often turn to diagrams when words fail us. The aim of this chapter is to help student teachers:

- to recognize the important different modes of communication in the learning of science;
- to monitor their own communications in the classroom;
- to increase their effective use of communication skills.

Introduction

How do you get to know what is in someone else's mind? The choice of strategies to obtain this information is rather limited. You can ask them to do something, to tell you something, to write it down or to draw a diagram. Science education makes use of all these modes. We ask pupils to do experiments, we discuss ideas with them and give them texts to read that include tables, charts and diagrams. We ask pupils to write and to draw their own ideas.

By asking pupils to tell us what they mean, to write it out in their own words, or to show us in a diagram, we are attempting to get the pupils to make public what is otherwise private. Only when the ideas are public can teachers then start to think more carefully about how they can help pupils develop their mental models for the natural phenomena being studied. The use of the term 'elicitation' might be preferred over the use of the word 'questioning' in this context. Science teachers need to elicit: to get pupils to make their ideas public. Public ideas can be shared and discussed, agreed, amended or abandoned.

Effective communication is a two-way street. This is true for communication in science education too. Just as teachers need to find out what pupils think so, too, pupils need to find out what science teachers, or scientists, think. Science teachers have a professional responsibility to monitor their own communication skills and to improve them consciously and deliberately. Activity 6.1 starts with boardwork: student teachers are asked to use the chalkboard, or whiteboard, and to practise their board skills, both diagrammatic and written. It is important they do this in advance of team-teaching parts of lessons when they will already need to have some basic skill. Student teachers' oral presentations are no less important than their use of the board. These are also touched on in activity 4.3, 'Explanation at the board/OHP'.

Activity 6.2 focuses on aural/oral work and discussion. The emphasis is on discussion and the elicitation of pupils' ideas. There are techniques, associated with managing a whole class discussion, that may traditionally have fallen under the heading of 'questioning techniques'. Much of the advice given under that heading is still very relevant. Here, with the emphasis on elicitation rather than questioning, the purpose of sharing of mental models is stronger than the purpose of finding out if the pupils know the 'right' answer.

Textual materials can form a substantial part of the resource teachers draw upon in helping pupils learn science. Activity 6.3a is concerned with reflecting on such materials and their use with different groups of pupils. Writing is undoubtedly more difficult than reading. An advantage of the written over the spoken is that pupils can review, evaluate and reform their written work before deciding that the final text is a correct account of their thoughts. With activity 6.3b, student teachers are invited to increase the range of writing tasks they set pupils. This will involve familiarization with a short menu of different styles of writing task and student teachers should use these different forms for pupils' writing activities, so they can evaluate how successful they may be in different contexts.

Activity 6.4 focuses on communication in forms other than text. Graphical, pictorial and numerical data are considered. The activity involves sharing perceptions of the student teacher's behaviour between the student teacher and an observer. These observations can be structured by using the suggested inventories.

In activity 6.5, Student teachers are asked to prepare written resources for use with pupils. This is an opportunity to draw together a wide range of different bits of knowledge and skill and should be incorporated into activity 4.5.

6.1 Boardwork

Mentor's Brief

Objective • The student teacher should be able to use the board to maximum effect.

Time   • When rooms are free and student teachers can practice.

Background

Good boardwork is one of the hallmarks of a good teacher. This is probably because the orderly mind of the good teacher is given expression in the orderly state of their boardwork. There may be a reflexive cause and effect in that trying to produce good boardwork will force the student teachers to order their thoughts and activities.

Instructions

- Suggest to the student teachers a topic that is imminent in the programme of study.
- Tell them to practise both diagrams and text at a chalkboard or whiteboard. They should use rooms that are free, or work before or at the end of the school day or during lunch.
- After a few days ask them to show you their boardwork.
- Be prepared to offer feedback and advice.

Discussion points

Using different media requires different approaches. The chalkboard, or whiteboard, is not the same as the OHP or printed page. OHP work requires its own techniques that are not simple extensions of boardwork. This warning is important. Generally people abuse the OHP by writing too much, in too small a hand, thereby negating one of the significant advantages of the OHP: the opportunity to change from one OHT to the next instantly. Word-processed OHTs are best kept to seven lines of text all at least of 24 point Times bold. Anything smaller is unreadable. It is an insult to the pupils to say, 'I know you can't read this but . . .' The general rule is that if it can't be read from the back of the room don't use it. OHTs can be used effectively to present information that is nested: where the first OHT displays the major headings that are then discussed in detail in a series of subsequent OHTs. The first OHT can be returned to at regular intervals to act as a signpost for progress through the presentation. OHTs can be prepared in advance. Good boardwork is more demanding on performance skills.

6.1 Boardwork

Student Teacher's Brief

Get to know your board: it is your most valuable tool. It will enable you to make the most complex topic simple. Think out your boardwork in

---

advance. With the board you can structure the pupils' concepts as you structure your presentation with headings, sub-headings, asides and illustrations. With the chalkboard you can start a lesson quietly even though the pupils have come in all hot and flustered from games, dance or drama. The chalkboard will enable you to bring the lesson to a timely and orderly close as pupils copy down a summary for, 'What we have done today' and their homework.

Objective

- You should be able to use the board to maximum effect.

Instructions

- Your mentor will suggest a topic that you can work on in terms of boardwork.
- Whenever you have some free time, between lesson observation sessions, at the end of the school day, find a free room and practise your boardwork.

- Start with written text. Adopt a style that you are comfortable with.
- Go to the furthest point in the room and check that pupils sitting at that point will be able to read your writing. Do this when you are working with the pupils too.
  Generally student teachers make the mistake of writing with too small a hand and writing too much on the board at any one time.

- When you have a hand that can be read from all points in the room turn your attention to the layout of what you are writing:
    Consider how best to use headings and sub-headings.
    Which information could go in boxes for highlighting.
    If you have a wide board should you write in columns? How many?
- Consider the possibility of partitioning the board so you have a section for text to be copied as best and a section for developing discussion points that arise.
- Get into the habit of going to the back of the room when one frame of work has been completed. This is a time when pupils will be copying and you can check on what they can see. It also helps to pace the activity by not moving on too rapidly.

- From the same topic, pick a diagram that you may wish to have on the board. Draw it up on the board.

Instructions

- Read through the example below.
- Find out from the teacher what the practical activity will be.
- Ask the teacher to suggest two rather different groups to work with.
  In the practical part of the lesson ask groups of pupils for their ideas.
  Work back and forth between the groups systematically.
- Immediately after the lesson, try to write a description of two of the groups that you have talked to, summarizing their main ideas at the different stages of the practical activity.
- Discuss your perceptions of the pupils' ideas of the practical activity with the teacher who took the lesson.
- Discuss with your mentor how you could modify your questions to help pupils develop their ideas.

Example

A practical activity often carried out by pupils in Year 8 involves heating a variety of substances and noting whether they change permanently, change temporarily or do not change at all. The main idea of the activity is to introduce pupils to physical and chemical change. The sorts of questions that the teacher can ask the pupils related to the different stages of the experiment are:

What do you expect to happen?
Tell me why?
Do you expect them all to behave in the same way? Why?
When you have seen other materials being heated did they all behave in similar ways or were there differences?
What were the differences?
Now I know what he thinks (addressed to a second pupil), can you tell me what you think?

Tell me how you should hold the test-tube whilst heating?
Why does it matter?
Why are you using this kind of Bunsen flame?
Do you (addressed to a second pupil) agree with that? why?

What do you see?
Anything else?
What do you hear?
What has happened to the solid at the bottom of the tube?
What about further up the tube?

How is this different from other substances that you have heated?
Why do you think that is?

How will you record your results?
Tell me why you have decided on that way
What will you write down?
What will you (addressed to a second pupil) be writing?

What patterns can you see in your results?
Which substances behave similarly/differently? In what ways?
Why do you think that some substances change permanently?
What is happening to them?
Why do you think that some substances change temporarily?
Is there anyone who disagrees with that? Can you tell me why?

How could you improve the experiment?
What would you like to investigate further?
Tell me how would you go about doing that?

6.2b Sharing Ideas

Mentor's Brief

Objective • Student teachers should have skills in sharing ideas in class by:
framing questions appropriately
Distributing questions around the class
Feeding positive comments back to pupils
Using eye-contact and positive body language.

Time • For the student teacher: spread over several weeks in preparation for team-teaching, teaching and feedback
• Observation and feedback, oral and written, for the mentor or
class teacher

Background

Student teachers can find it particularly difficult to develop effective questioning skills. In this particular area the differences between novices and experienced professional teachers can be striking. Novices exhibit the following
characteristics:

• They are more concerned about transmitting information to pupils
and less aware of the need to monitor pupils' learning. Consequently
they tend to tell the pupils too much and do not ask enough questions.

- Most questions tend to be used to elicit short responses which are mainly factual recall. Pupils have fewer opportunities to explain their ideas.
- In novices' classes, pupils seem to get the wrong answer more often, and student teachers tend to be less adept at accepting an incorrect answer or an unclear answer and getting pupils to expand on the answer and explain their thinking.
- Their management of questioning sessions is less well controlled: rules for answering questions are less clearly defined and questions tend not to distributed around the whole class.

Like riding a bicycle, helping pupils to share their ideas requires several teacher skills at the same time. Even though bicycle riding skills can be separated analytically into balance, confidence, motion, they cannot be separated practically. The same is true for helping pupils share ideas. Four questioning skills are identified in this activity: framing, distributing, feeding back and using body language. Effective questioning involves each of these skills at the same time.

At this stage in the student teacher's development, an observer is needed for each lesson. The information about these skills must then be fed into the student teacher's planning for later lessons. When using a new skill, teachers sometimes use it effectively at the beginning of the lesson, but then become absorbed in other aspects of running a lesson and forget to use the new skill.

Instructions

- Select lessons for the student teacher to team-teach where the student teacher has to use elicitation skills for the sharing of ideas. Combine this activity with activity 4.2c, 'Demonstrations with questions and answers'.

After the lesson you, or a colleague who has been watching the lesson, need to provide the student teacher with oral and written feedback (refer to the notes in Chapter 1, Action 3: Debriefing).

- First the observations are fed back to the student-teacher.
  No value judgments are made at this stage; this stage is purely descriptive.
- Next the student-teacher is asked to reflect on his/her own performance.
- Finally the discussion focuses around the most appropriate style of questioning. This will vary according to the pupils being taught, what is being taught, how it is being taught, etc. There is no single best way of questioning. Often, however, there are better ways.

When the student teacher has progressed to teaching complete lessons it will still be useful to provide feedback on their questioning skills.

6.2b   Sharing Ideas

Student Teacher's Brief

Research shows that pupils' ideas are seldom congruent with those of the teacher. It would be naive to think it could be otherwise: for pupils are pupils precisely because they do not know what the teacher knows. Using elicitation with pupils allows you to bring their thinking into the public arena where it can be shared by others. If one pupil thinks something, it is quite likely that others will have similar ideas.

Objective

You should be able to use the following skills with oral elicitations in class:

- Framing questions appropriately
- Distributing questions around the class
- Feeding positive comments back to pupils
- Using eye-contact and positive body language

Instructions

- Your mentor will ask you to team-teach parts of lessons that involve demonstrations or explanations.
- Refer to activity 4.2 on managing explanations and demonstrations.
- Read the following notes before planning your part in the lessons.

Notes on sharing ideas

The framing of questions
There are three components to planning before the lesson:

- Goals
- Starting points
- Routes.

Be clear on the main ideas that you would like the pupils to know and use at the end of the lesson. Have tactics for finding out what pupils

---

already know and can use. Consider the sequence in which you might develop the sub-topics. You will need to think how you can break questions down into simpler questions or how you can rephrase them if pupils find them difficult.

The following techniques can be useful in encouraging pupils to contribute:

- Have a stimulus that poses a problem;
- When pupils give answers you can encourage them to talk more;
- Give the pupils enough time to think;
- Keep a written record of pupil involvement by extracting some key words from a pupil's answer and write them on the board;
- Keep your focus by making the question and answer sessions relatively short.

If you want to discuss the factors affecting plant growth you could begin by presenting the pupils with two sets of seedlings, one of which has been grown in a dark cupboard and one which has been grown by a window. Ask the pupils what differences they notice. This allows all the pupils to be immediately engaged. Follow up by asking them why they thought there were these differences. Ask, 'Why do you say that?' or, 'Can you explain a bit more?' Repeat the last sentence that the pupil has said and pause to encourage elaboration. Sometimes teachers ask a question; pause; wait for pupils to put up their hands; repeat the question; and wait a bit longer before asking a pupil to give an answer. Ask other pupils for their ideas on key words written on the board. You can also use these in a summary and it adds value to pupils' contributions. Ten minutes without a break is probably long enough for most classes.

Distributing questions around the class
The aim of distributing questions around the class is to involve as many pupils as possible in active participation in the lesson. Aspects to consider on maximizing participation are the following:

- The rules that you establish for answering questions.
- The physical position of a pupil in the classroom.
- Whether the pupil is identifiably from some group: boys/girls; working class/middle class; ethnic origins; extrovert/withdrawn; and so on.

The following are useful in helping you interact with the class more equitably:

- Tell the pupils your rules for answering questions.
- Direct questions all around the room from the start. Do not allow no-go areas to develop.

- Do not ask only pupils whose hand are up.
- Consciously reposition yourself around the room.
- Ask a colleague to observe you and provide feedback.
- Operate the school procedures for enforcing your rules.

When infringed, as your rules will be, repeat them. Most effective teachers do not allow pupils to call out answers. They select pupils to answer questions, wait for pupils to put their hands up and then select pupils systematically. Be aware that the dynamics of pupil involvement depend upon where the teacher stands. Move down the sides of the room. Standing at the back can be a useful place from which to direct questioning. Boys often demand more attention than girls and so it is useful to consider this when directing questions. Even experienced teachers find it difficult to resist the pressures of some pupils. Having a colleague observe and discuss the pattern of your elicitations will help you to become more pro-active and less re-active.

Giving positive feedback
Pupils are encouraged if they get positive feedback. Do say:

> 'Well done'
> 'Good answer'
> 'Good try'

You can also give encouragement by your facial expression. One way in which student teachers differ from experienced teachers is in how they respond to pupils' partially correct answers. Experienced teachers will do the following:

- Ask pupils to rephrase their answers, or say a bit more about it;
- Pick out part of an answer and ask pupils to expand on it;
- Rephrase the question and give the pupil another opportunity to answer;
- Ask other pupils what they think of other pupil's answers.

Eye contact and body language
There are two separate situations where eye-contact is useful:

- During discussion scan the room and make sure that you engage pupils' eyes. This has the effect of promoting your interaction with them personally. A lack of eye-contact can lead to disengagement and off-task activity;
- Pupils who are straying from the main activity can be shepherded back through eye-contact that lets them know that you know what's going on.

You will probably need to move around the room to make sure that you maintain eye-contact with wayward pupils. The small trouble of doing this can save you a lot greater effort if you fail to do it.

You transmit a message by the way you stand and walk as well as through how you talk. Ask a colleague to give you honest feedback on your body language. Better still, arrange to have your part in lessons video-taped so that you can see how others see you.

6.3a   Assessing Materials for Differentiated Reading Skills

Mentor's Brief

Objective   •   The student teacher should report on the suitability of the textual resources used in the science department.

Time   •   3 hours for student teachers to review various texts and write a brief report
   • $\frac{1}{2}$ hour discussion with mentor

Instructions

•   Direct the student teacher to the written resources used in the department.
   They will need to look at texts used with Years 7, 9, 11 and perhaps sixth-form texts. They will also need access to the science materials used to support non-readers and that for pupils for whom English is a second language (ESL).
•   Briefly discuss the review task with the student teacher.
   They might do this activity as a prelude to activity 4.4 on reviewing a scheme of work.
•   Discuss the student teacher's report.

6.3a   Assessing Materials for Differentiated Reading Skills

Student Teacher's Brief

Reading is important for pupils in science lessons. Pupils can access information and activities independently if they can read. However reading performance is not an on/off switch. Pupils can be differentiated along an extended scale according to the texts they can cope with. Certain features of text can hinder pupils' access to the information in the text. A well designed text can help them.

Objective

You should report on the suitability of the textual resources used in the science department in your school.

Instructions

- Your mentor will direct you to a range of texts used in the department.
- Read the notes on text given below.
- Write a brief report on the department's textual resources and their suitability for the pupils concerned.

Notes on textual material

These are things to pay attention to when reviewing textual resources:

- The layout and design of a text can be the most enabling/inhibiting feature:
  - Texts with a good proportion of white-space to print are easier to access.
  - The positioning of diagrams and illustrations is important in helping pupils gain maximum benefit from the information.
  - Starting new ideas on new lines makes the absorption of those ideas easier. (What do you think of the layout and design in this book? Does it help you? How/how not?)
- Sentence length can also change the accessibility of a text:
  - Generally, the shorter the sentences the easier the text is to read.
  - Sentences that start with the subject are easier to read.
  - Long sentences with lots of commas and clauses are very difficult and often need re-reading.
- The sequencing of ideas/sentences so that they follow the chronological flow of actions is helpful to readers
  - descriptions that start globally and work down to detail are also easier to visualize.

- The careful choice of verb tenses can improve the readability considerably:

    Passive forms are more difficult to interpret than active forms.

- The vocabulary of science is specialized:

    Science uses everyday words but with meanings that are different from everyday usage.

    Scientific terms have precise meanings and are often difficult to pronounce and spell. However, surprisingly, this turns out to be one of the least important aspects of what makes text difficult for pupils.

6.3b Alternative Writing Activities for Pupils

Mentor's Brief

Objective • Student teachers should know of different forms of writing that might be used to achieve different purposes in science education. They should be able to use them with their classes so as to evaluate them.

Time • Reading time and lesson time for the student teacher
• $\frac{1}{2}$ hour discussion with mentor

Background

The results of science, hot from the laboratory, are written-up as papers for specialist journals and conference proceedings. The forerunner of the journal, before learned societies took over the dissemination of their members' scientific information, was the private letter. Today science is written about in popular magazines like New Scientist and Focus. Newspapers often carry articles that have a scientific component interpreted for the general public by journalists. Scientists themselves have been known to write songs, poems and limericks with scientific content.

Many science teachers have made efforts to move away from the echo of the scientific paper that is found in the standard format of, Aim, Apparatus, Method or Procedure, Results, Analysis and Conclusions, which had a stranglehold on science education in the past. If student teachers have not been exposed to thinking about other forms of writing it is unlikely they will come to it spontaneously. This activity introduces them to different modes of writing and how they might be incorporated as pupils' activities in lesson plans and schemes of work.

Instructions

- Collect several examples of different kinds of writing done by pupils in past science lessons. Give them to the student teacher to read.
- Direct the student teacher to the Programmes of Study of Science in the National Curriculum and focus their attention on comments on pupils' written work.
- Discuss the possible roles of writing in science lessons, including the role of a formal scientific report, with the student teacher.
- Ask the student teacher to select a variety of different writing styles to use in different science lessons, and discuss the value of these after the student teacher has tried them with a class.

Discussion points

The discussions with student teachers should centre on the purposes and opportunities for learning through different forms of writing. A discussion on the matching of activities to aims and objectives might help structure the conversation.

6.3b   Alternative Writing Activities for Pupils

Student Teacher's Brief

Objective

- You should know of different forms of writing that might be used to achieve different purposes in science education. You should be able to use them with your classes so as to evaluate different forms of writing.

Instructions

- Read the selection of different forms of writing given to you by your mentor.
- Write down why you think the pupils have been asked to write in the different styles.
  Who was the perceived audience?
  What was the purpose of writing in this way?
  How might this activity have helped the pupils' learning of science?
  When, in a scheme of work, might be the best time to do this type of activity?

- Review the Programmes of Study for Key Stages 3 and 4 of Science in the National Curriculum. What forms of writing are suggested?
- Discuss your studies with your mentor.
- Plan to use a selection of different forms of writing in lessons that you teach. Several ideas are given below.
- After you have used a form of writing that is new to you, study the pupils' writing and decide:
    > whether your aims in using this form of writing have been achieved
    > whether the pupils found a different way of writing motivating.
- Discuss this with your mentor.

Ideas for forms of writing:

- A letter to another scientist in a different country
- A poem
- An account for a teenagers' magazine
- A TV reporter's script for a newscast
- A limerick
- A diary entry by a scientists in the seventeenth century
- A telegram
- An account in *The Guardian* newspaper
- An account in *The Sun* newspaper
- A song
- The script for a conversation in the *Dr Who* science fiction TV programme

Pupils will appreciate being able to read one another's accounts. You can provide a regularly changing wall display of pupils' work which will brighten-up and personalize the laboratory and classroom. If this activity is taken seriously by you it can become motivating for pupils.

Examples of pupils' poems

- 14-year-old girl starting on *Nuffield Co-ordinated Science*:

Rocks

and plants can

generously sustain our life

chemically. If we do not know

their worth it's good-bye

to life on

Earth

- 16-year-old boy doing separate science physics:
  Each time it passed the lamp, you see,
  the electron gave its energy,
  The battery thought this was rather poor,
  The electron returned for more and more.
  Round and round at a steady pace
  It was an endless race.
- 16-year-old girl doing separate science biology:
  How can a pea
  be like me
  genetically?
  It has two parents.
  So do I.
  Its chromosomes are rather shy,
  they hide inside its nuclei.
  Its father's traits and mother's too
  have left it with a hue of blue.
  My eyes are too.
- 12-year-old girl doing 'Minibeasts':
  Underneath the trees there is a world in itself.
  Minibeasts forage for food.
  Who is predator and who is prey?
  This is what we looked at today.
  We had to stop.
  Lunch was on its way.

6.4 Pictures, numbers and graphs

Mentor's Brief

Objective • Student teachers should be able to reflect on how they help
pupils improve their diagrammatic, numerical and graphical
communication skills and consider how to amend lesson plans
accordingly.

Time • 10 minutes at the end of various lessons for the student teacher
• $\frac{1}{2}$ hour discussion with the mentor

Background

The inventories in the student teacher activity here will have a familiar ring
to teachers who know of the taxonomy of cognitive skills described in *A
Taxonomy of Educational Objectives: Handbook* 1 (Bloom, *et al.*, 1956). The focusing on pupils' actions helps to guide the selection of learning activities. Most
of the actions for pupils described in the inventories have some translation

component. That is, pupils have to describe things orally or in written accounts. By telling, or writing, about what a particular mode of representation is being used to represent, pupils are making public, twice over, their communication. Reflexively, they can use the one to enhance the other.

By this means mathematics enters science as a way of communicating information in a succinct and precise way. The mathematics should grow naturally out of a need to communicate the science efficiently and effectively.

Instructions

- Direct the student teacher to the inventories in the activity.
- Check occasionally that the student teacher is reflecting on the opportunities they are providing for pupils to develop their communication skills.
- Discuss with the student teacher the pupils' progression in communication skills.
- Set targets for the student teacher to plan more effective activities that develop communication skills in pupils.

Discussion points

The three inventories provided here can be used as a quarry for behavioural objectives for pupils in working with different modes of communication.

The work in Chapter 9 on Piagetian stages in cognitive progression should alert student teachers to the way in which pupils may show differentiated performance on the items in these inventories. The inventories can be used to plan objectives and activities that may encourage accelerated progression in pupils' cognitive skills.

6.4 Pictures, Numbers and Graphs

Student Teacher's Brief

Objective

- You should reflect on how you help pupils improve their diagrammatic, numerical and graphical communication skills and consider how to amend your lesson plans accordingly.

Instructions

- Complete a communications inventory immediately after teaching a lesson.
- Do this with several lessons so as to get a broader picture of how you are teaching.

- Find items in the inventory for which you are not providing pupils with activities at the moment.
- Consider how you should modify your lesson plans to incorporate more opportunities for pupils to increase their communication skills.
- Discuss your plans with your mentor.

An inventory for diagrammatic communication

In which lessons have you helped pupils to develop their communication skills in using diagrams by having activities which require pupils to carry out the following actions?

- Reproduction
    copying a diagram
    reproducing a diagram from memory
- Translation
    describing a complete diagram orally
    writing a description of a diagram
- Interpretation
    explaining the link between form and function or operation orally
    writing an explanation linking form, function and operation.

An inventory for numerical communication

In which lessons have you helped pupils to develop their communication skills in using numbers by having activities which require pupils to carry out the following actions?

- Displaying numerical information by pupils
    selecting a suitable tabular form
    selecting suitable headings
    selecting suitable units
    completing cell entries systematically
    completing cell entries with precision
- Translating of information from numerical form by pupils
    describing trends in numbers orally
    using trends to complete missing entries
    writing a description of the trends in numbers
    interpreting the trends in terms of variables
- Transforming numerical data to obtain further information
    hypothesizing relationships
    suggesting suitable transformations of data
    carrying out transformations systematically
    using transformations to confirm hypotheses

An inventory for graphical communication

In which lessons have you helped pupils to develop their communication skills in using graphs by having activities which require pupils to carry out the following actions?

- Describing the shape of a line or curve, pie chart or bar chart
    pupils giving an oral description
    pupils writing a description of the shape of a graph
- Hypothesizing possible shapes of line or curve, pie chart or bar chart
    reviewing alternatives for the phenomenon being studied
    arguing for one shape, rather than another, for the phenomenon being studied
- Preparing to plot graphs or charts
    pupils selecting an appropriate size for the units
    pupils selecting units
    pupils selecting dependent/independent variables
    pupils selecting variables
- Interpreting from a graph
    given an 'x' value finding a 'y' value
    given 'y' value finding an 'x' value
    extrapolating a graph beyond the data set
    predicting a new curve when a controlled parameter is changed, and thereby produces a parallel set of results, e.g. rate of production of carbon dioxide in sugar solutions of different concentrations at different temperatures.
- Formalizing the relationship between the variables represented in the graph in an algebraic form
    recognizing the shape of the curve in terms of a general equation
    writing a specific equation for the graphical information presented
    using the equation produced to make a prediction.
    checking the prediction made algebraically against the data represented in the graph.

6.5 Designing Text-based Resources

Mentor's Brief

Objective • The student teacher should produce a good quality text-based resource for trialling and revision.

Time
- 3 hours for the student teacher to write a worksheet, trial, evaluate
- $\frac{1}{2}$ hour discussion with mentor

Background

Activity 3.3a considers textual resources. DARTs are introduced and student teachers are directed to constructing DARTs of their own design. DARTs are particularly useful for language and concept development. Activity 8.3 is also concerned with textual resources. The focus is in terms of the introduction of a historical perspective.

In this activity student teachers can be given a free hand to produce text-based resources that would be suitable for inclusion in a revised scheme of work. This ties in with activities 4.4 and then 4.5: reviewing and revising part of a scheme of work. The opportunity for creativity on the part of the student teacher and the advantage of having carefully planned activities for pupils can provide stimulus. The activity has been delayed to this stage of a student teacher's development because he or she will, by now, have used a wide variety of other text-based resources and will have formed opinions on what works and what does not.

Teachers can be rushed when writing worksheets and the quality often suffers as a result. In this activity the student teacher is given time to produce a high quality resource. Student teachers should be encouraged to produce as good a quality text-based resource as the school's reprographics and software will allow.

Instructions

- Suggest the topic area in which the student teacher might compile a text-based pupil activity sheet. This could be the same as that for the review and revision of part of a scheme of work (activities 4.4 and 4.5).
- If activity 3.3c was not carried out earlier now is another chance to do so. Help may be required in the technical aspects of word processing and use of graphics packages.
- Review the text-based resource and suggest improvements.
- The student teacher should trial the text-based resource in a lesson.
- Discuss the trialling with the student teacher.

Discussion points

The work required to produce one good quality text-based resource is substantial. Student teachers may appreciate the usefulness of working as a team to develop resources when they have carried out this work.

6.5 Designing Text-based Resources

Student Teacher's Brief

This activity provides you with an opportunity to be creative and produce text-based resources that will help you in the classroom with pupils' activities.

- You will need to draw upon your experience of using a wide range of books, papers and worksheets with pupils.
- Reflect on what is attractive to look at and therefore motivating for pupils – think carefully about the placement of illustration.
- Try to structure the pupils' activities so that all pupils can succeed in the earlier stages of using the resource. Think about how activities that come later in the text might have progression built into them. Refer to activities 9.4 and 9.5 on cognitive growth and differentiation.
- If you did not complete activity 3.3c on IT and are not familiar with word-processing or the use of graphics packages for the machines in your school, then now is the time to make sure you correct that deficiency.

Objective

- You should produce a good quality text-based resource for trialling and revision.

Instructions

- Carry out this activity as part of your work for activities 4.4 and 4.5.
- Review your notes from activity 6.4a.
- Design a new resource or improve one that is already written.
- Show the text-based resource to your mentor or another teacher and ask for comments. Revise the resource if necessary.
- Try out the resource in your lesson. Revise it if necessary.
- Discuss the trial with your mentor.

Chapter 7

Science and Knowledge

Aims

Most scientists would claim that a scientific approach to the study of natural phenomena produces reliable knowledge. But many student science teachers start their science-teaching careers without giving a serious thought to the question, 'What is scientific knowledge and how is it made?' The aims of the activities in this chapter are to help student teachers:

- think about the nature of science itself;
- think about how their views of the nature of science might influence which activities they select for learners;
- develop strategies for organizing work across age groups and abilities that match selected approaches to science.

Introduction

Science teachers regularly ask pupils to make novel observations. To the non-scientist, this appears to be the starting place for how science makes new reliable knowledge. A scientist's work might be interpreted as simply looking at the natural world that little bit harder and more carefully than ordinary folk. However, without having ideas about what is being observed, is this possible? Lewis Wolpert (1992) is one recent commentator who points out that if ideas are common sense then they are probably not scientific. In activity 7.1, student teachers are asked to think about whether the science in a natural phenomenon is self-evident and how teachers manage pupils' observations.

In activity 7.2a, students teachers take a scientific concept with which they think they are familiar and reconstruct the principal justifications for a belief in its validity. In activity 7.2b, they plan a scheme of activities that could be used to lead pupils through the steps in developing an understanding of the same concept.

Science involves scientists making new knowledge through the use of processes or methods. Learning science has a component that is about mastering these processes of knowledge making. Activity 7.3 involves student teachers in planning learning experiences that help pupils rehearse and thereby strengthen their skills in using those processes.

Although there are many different varieties of scientist and scientific work, scientists share common beliefs in the need to produce results that are reproducible, significant, usually explicable with some material mechanism, ideally numerical and thereby capable of being used to make precise predictions. Activity 7.4 involves student teachers considering if these aims are reflected in what they teach and in the way that they teach it. Finally in activity 7.5, student teachers are invited to complete a questionnaire and thereby to consider their own personal stance towards science and their opinion on what 'doing science' and 'being scientific' means.

7.1 Managing Observing

Mentor's Brief

Objective • Student teachers should be able to use ideas from their study of the way science makes new knowledge to look critically at the way pupils are encouraged to build their scientific knowledge from observations.

Time • 3 or 4 lessons with practical or demonstration work for the student teacher to team teach and observe
• $\frac{1}{2}$ hour discussion with mentor

Background

How science makes new knowledge and the status of that knowledge is open to debate. It is a debate that has been long running and continues to have new ideas injected into it. This activity is not an attempt to provide student teachers with a definitive answer. It is intended that student teachers should be alert to the fact that they can help pupils improve their observations by structuring the learning experience managerially and thereby pedagogically. This intention has a respectable pedigree in that it was one of the concerns of Michael Faraday as a lecturer at the Friday Evening Discourses at the Royal Institution.

Instructions

• Select science lessons with practical or demonstration activities in them.
• Student teachers should be directed to observe demonstrations and practicals in science lessons and report back on instances where pupils were involved in making observations of natural phenomena.
• Discuss the student teacher's observations.

Keep the conversation focused on the pedagogic support and managerial strategies for helping pupils observe natural phenomena. The philosophical issues can be left for discussion elsewhere.

The visibility of the scale on the meters, the size of the effects to be seen by the pupils, the placing of the pupils are all within the teacher's control.

This is one place where modern technology can be easily introduced into science lessons but is still sadly lacking. In demonstrations, if apparatus, organism or effect is small and difficult to see, use a TV camera and a TV monitor so that the whole class has a view.

7.1 Managing Observing

Student Teacher's Brief

In this activity you are to watch science classes and pay attention to the way in which pupils are asked to make observations of natural phenomena, either during demonstrations or when pupils are carrying out their own investigations.

Objective

You should be able to use ideas from the study of the way science makes new knowledge to look critically at the way pupils are encouraged to build their scientific knowledge from their own observations.

Instructions

- Read the extracts below, from *Advice to a Lecturer* by Michael Faraday (1960).
- Agree with your mentor which lessons you should observe as you team-teach.
- When pupils are involved in observational work take note of the following issues:

  (i) Issues of what type of thing is being observed, like:
  things that can be directly sensed, seen, smelt, felt, heard, etc., such as forces, colours.
  things that are construed such as structural, anatomical or morphological features.
  things that are construed and accessible through instrumentation, ammeters, microscopes, pH meters, etc. such as current, osmotic potential and hydrogen ion concentration.

Consider the difference between:

> description in answer to the question, 'What is happening?' and explanation, in answer to the question, 'Why is it happening?'

and the relative difficulties pupils have with these.

(ii) In the classroom, observational issues are structured by pedagogic issues, like:

> how do the teachers introduce an observation activity for the pupils?
>
> are pupils encouraged to make untutored observations?
>
> are initial observations discussed with the class as a whole?
>
> does the discussion lead to a consensus on what all might observe?
>
> do the pupils return to make tutored observations?
>
> the sequencing of parts of demonstrations so that pupils are moved smoothly from considering the 'what' to the 'why' of the phenomenon.

(iii) In turn these are underpinned by managerial issues, like:

> where teachers place demonstrations for pupils to watch.
>
> what teachers do to group and move pupils so they can see.
>
> the use of big, bold demonstrations where effects are demonstrable.
>
> the distribution and use of open questions that cannot be answered with just a 'yes' or 'no' but require an opinion or observation.

- Discuss your observations with your mentor.

Extracts from, Advice to a Lecturer *by Michael Faraday*

Consider the advice given by Faraday on lectures and think about how it may also apply to any observation work carried out by pupils.

> An experimental lecturer should attend very carefully to the choice he may make of his experiments for the illustration of his subject. They should be important, as they respect the science they are applied to, yet clear and such as may easily be understood.

> They should rather approach to simplicity and explain the established principles of the subject than elaborate and apply to minute phenomena only. . . . Let your experiments apply to the subject you elucidate, and do not introduce those that are not to the point.

Neither should too much stress be laid on what I would call small experiments, or rather illustrations. It pleases me well to observe a neat idea enter the head of a lecturer which he will immediately and aptly illustrate or explain by a few motions of his hand — a card, a lamp, a glass of water or any other things that may be near him . . .

'Tis well too when the lecturer has the ready wit and presence of mind to turn any casual circumstances that has become table-talk for the town, any local advantages or disadvantages, any trivial circumstances that may arise in company, give great force to the illustrations drawn from them, and please the audience highly as they conceive they perfectly understand them.

Apparatus, therefore is an essential part of every lecture in which it can be introduced; but to apparatus should be added at every convenient opportunity illustrations that may not perhaps deserve the name of apparatus and experiments, and yet may be introduced with considerable force and effect in proper places.

Diagrams and tables too are necessary, or at least add in an eminent degree to the illustration and perfection of a lecture. When an experimental lecture is to be delivered and apparatus is to be exhibited, some kind of order should be preserved in the arrangement of them on the lecture table. Every particulate part illustrative of the lecture should be in view; no one thing should hide another from the audience, nor should anything stand in the way of the lecturer.

Diagrams, tho' ever so rough, are often times of important use in a lecture. The facility with which they illustrate ideas and the diversity they produce in circumstances occurant (*sic*) render them highly agreeable to an audience. By diagrams I do not mean drawings (nor do I exclude drawings) but a plain and simple statement in a few lines of what requires many words. A sheet of cartridge paper and a pen or a blackboard and chalk are often times of great importance. I in general allude to temporary diagrams and would resort to temporary means to obtain them.

A diagram or a table (by which I mean constituent parts or proportions written out in a rough enlarged way) should be left in the view of the audience for a short time after the lecturer himself has explained that they may arrange the ideas contained in them in their minds and also refer to them in any other parts of the theory connected with the same subject and (if they choose, as is often the case) also to copy them.

7.2a How do we Know?

Mentor's Brief

Objective • Student teachers should be made aware of how they take knowledge for granted and how their pupils may not share that knowledge.

Time • 1 hour for the student teacher to research and write
• 20 minutes discussion with mentor

Background

Evidence does not speak for itself. It needs a theoretical interpreter. This is all the more so when, in the course of scientific enquiry, people investigate natural phenomena that are beyond simple sensory experience and where the arrival at secure knowledge requires mathematical manipulation of data.

Instructions

• Student teachers should be asked to pick some concept in science and carefully re-construct the principal justifications for a belief in the validity of that concept.
• An account of the size of atomic nuclei might start with the pattern of scattering of alpha particles by gold nuclei. An account of why we believe DNA to have a helical structure will be sure to include the patterns of scattered X-rays. Any account of why we accept the electronic structure of the atom will have to include reference to the empirical evidence of spectra.

Discussion points

Student teachers can be surprised by their own ignorance of the interplay between empirical evidence and scientific theory. To re-create the sense of bemusement and partial understanding that many pupils suffer, it may be worth pointing the student teachers to a topic that is not part of their own specialism in science. This may need the co-operation of colleagues.

7.2a How do we Know?

Student Teacher's Brief

Objective

You should be aware of how you take knowledge for granted and how your pupils may not share that knowledge.

Instructions

- Pick a topic from your knowledge of science and re-trace the evidence that leads us to believe that the currently accepted account is reasonable.

  You may pick topics such as knowledge of the size of atomic nuclei, the helical structure of DNA; or the electronic structure of the atom.

  How can it be shown, step-by-step, that these accounts are justifiable?

  What evidence persuades the community of scientists to accept these ideas? Empirical evidence is obviously important, but that empirical evidence has to be interpreted in the light of theory.

  What is the interplay between evidence and theory for the topic you pick?

  - Write a brief account of 'how we know'.

  In your written account you should consider if it would be possible to arrive at such conclusions without any theory.

  Can the evidence speak for itself or does it need theoretical interpreter?

7.2b Sequencing Conceptual Development

Mentor's Brief

Objective • Student teachers should be able to sequence a set of activities for pupils that take pupils from sensory experience to more abstract concepts.

Time • 2 hours for the student teacher to research and write
 • $\frac{1}{2}$ hour discussion with mentor

Instructions

- Discuss the activity with the student teacher
- Review their suggested set of activities for pupils.

Discussion points

The interplay between empirical evidence and theoretical construct can be developed here in the student teacher's scheme. You may wish to comment on:

- the need to start with sensory experiences
- the need to ask open questions of pupils about those experiences
- how teachers need to inject the scientific viewpoint into the discussion
- how teachers can formalise a consensus view for the class
- the need for pupils to have written accounts of their work.

7.2b Sequencing Conceptual Development

Student Teacher's Brief

Objective

You should be able to sequence a set of activities for pupils that take pupils from sensory experience to more abstract concepts.

Instructions

You are going to plan a sequence of demonstrations, or practical hands-on experiences, for pupils that will lead them from direct sensory experience to more derived abstract concepts. For example, in developing the concept of 'refraction' of light one might want pupils to do the following:

Have the experience of looking at objects through spectacles to see that what is seen through the spectacle lens is not identical with what is seen unaided.

Pupils might then be given the opportunity to do a ray box experiments in which the deviation of the paths of rays of light passing through lenses can be observed.

This might lead onto an experiment with a parallel-sided glass block where the amount of bending of the light is considered more carefully and in a controlled way.

Ripple tank demonstrations would be a sensible suggestion for the next activity so that pupils can see how water waves also change direction when they move into areas of different depths of water.

Pupils might then experience how light is deviated as it passes though prisms of different shapes.

This could be followed by a return to the ripple tank to see the effect with glass plates at the bottom of the tank being used as an analogue for the prism.

- Pick one topic like those listed here:

acceleration	rate of reaction	ecosystem
pressure	concentration	excretion
potential difference	oxidation	homeostasis
electric field	half-life	community
latent heat	electronic structure	photosynthesis

- Write out your demonstrations and practical experiences for pupils.

  You will find that you will need to add in theoretical ideas that can be used to explain observations in your demonstrations and experiments.
- Discuss your sequence of activities with your mentor.

7.3 Issues of Process

Mentor's Brief

Objective
- Student teachers should be able to design a set of activities for pupils for a topic in science that take the pupils through the processes of science.

Time
- 3 hours for the student teacher to work on researching and designing
- $\frac{1}{2}$ hour discussion with mentor

Background

There is a saying that has been popularized by Oxfam, amongst other aid agencies, 'Give a person a fish and you feed them for a day. Teach the person to fish and you feed them for life.' A somewhat similar statement could be made about science education. Teach a person content and they know how to deal with one topic. Teach a person process and they know how to do science. To become scientific, rather than simply knowing some science, is to augment your knowledge making potential.

Instructions

- Student teachers should be asked to focus on specific processes of science as part of their routine lesson planning.
- Monitor the student teachers' planning to make sure that they understand the purpose of the activity.
- Review the student teachers' set of activities based on processes and suggest improvements.

Discussion points

There are two points to make in talking with student teachers. Firstly, these activities present the knowledge-making processes of science in an atomistic way which contrasts with the more holistic viewpoint taken in Chapter 5 'Science Investigations'. The assumption here is that individual processes can be isolated and pupils' skill is susceptible to training. The atomism is softened if individual processes are linked through them having content, or topic, in common. Secondly, many of the processes can involve pupils in pencil and paper or discussion activities. They need not be practical.

7.3 Issues of Process

Student Teacher's Brief

Investigations, are dealt with in Chapter 5, and are an important component of being more scientific. Chapter 5 concentrates on the planning, organizational and managerial aspects of investigations: the structuring of lessons and the raising of pupils' levels of performance. The approach is holistic: an investigation is dealt with as a complete unit. This activity focuses on the internal workings of making new knowledge through operating the processes of science. It is therefore more atomistic. Rarely outside science do we carry out complete scientific investigations. However we often make hypotheses, we may weigh evidence and occasionally we formulate models. We use individual processes of knowledge making in science. In daily life, the conscious awareness of how we are operating such processes can help to improve our judgment.

In making new knowledge, scientists carry out actions that have common patterns. These actions that are common to science are identified as the processes of science. Below is a set of processes of science. They are not the only set possible nor necessarily an exhaustive set but they do reflect many of the features of science.

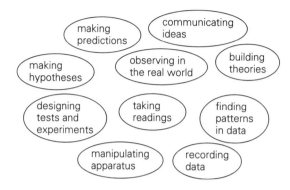

Figure 7.1: A possible set of processes in science

Objective

You should be able to design a set of activities for pupils for a topic in science that take the pupils through the processes of science.

Instructions

- Read the notes below on possible pupils' activities for processes involved in making scientific knowledge.
- Pick a topic in science, possibly one of those listed below, and plan activities for pupils that will help them develop some of the processes of science in the above set.

adaptation and survival	properties of elements	electrical conduction
genetic variation	states of matter	conservation of energy
predator–prey relationships	effects of electrolysis	dynamics of bodies

- Discuss your proposed activities with your mentor.

Notes on possible pupils' activities for processes involved in making scientific knowledge

Noticing patterns in the real world
This has to be some form of demonstration or exploratory practical work.

Making hypotheses
During a demonstration this could be carried out orally. With exploratory experiments it might be followed up with small group discussions and writing.

Designing a test or experiment

Pupils could be encouraged to work in groups. Their product might be presented orally or a writing and drawing exercise could be used. Such design activities do not necessarily have to be for experiments the pupils will carry out. The content of the topic can form a basis for the activity but the focus can be on training pupils in designing tests and experiments.

Observing and measuring

Pupils need to be given the opportunity to take measurements from instruments or to make original observations. With the focus of the pupil's activity on taking readings it is possible to train pupils by providing them with pre-set instruments in a circus of stations. This can be related to the experiments they have designed and tried but does not have to be at the same time that they carry out their experiments.

Finding patterns in data

This can be a pencil and paper activity where pupils work from data that is provided on a worksheet. Again this does not have to be the data they collect in their own experiments. Pupils can both learn content and be trained in this process as a single activity.

Building theories

Pupils should be asked to devise theories for why the phenomenon under study occur. This is not the same as describing the phenomenon. From the work in activity 7.1 you should know that explaining 'why' is much more difficult than saying 'what'. This activity provides a useful springboard for introducing scientists thoughts about why the phenomenon occurs. This is the point to teach some content. It is also an opportunity to contextualize the scientists' ideas with some activities on the history of science. See activity 8.3.

7.4 Criteria for Acceptability of Scientific Knowledge

Mentor's Brief

Objective   • Student teachers should be able to comment on the way pupils' learning of science reflects the values and beliefs scientists themselves use to judge the acceptability of scientific knowledge.

Time   • 3 hours for the student teacher reviewing, analysing and writing
    • $\frac{1}{2}$ hour discussion with mentor

Instructions

- Give the student teacher a scheme of work which involves a significant amount of practical work. This is best if incorporated into activity 4.4.
- The student teacher analyses the material for evidence of implicit or explicit values.
- Discuss the results of the review and analysis with the student teacher.

Discussion points

With junior and lower secondary science, the constraints of these five criteria, set out at the start of the student teacher's brief, are weak and pupil investigations are generally more spontaneous and enjoyable. It is the gradual strengthening of the constraint of the criteria that can make learning science less spontaneous, more like professional science, and perhaps less enjoyable. However, the reduction of enjoyment in upper secondary science might, in part, be attributable to these five criteria being latent and not made explicit by teachers. Pupils can be encouraged if helped to see themselves developing their science skills through explicit discussion of these criteria.

7.4 Criteria for Acceptability of Scientific Knowledge

Student Teacher's Brief

Here is a set of five values or beliefs, providing criteria for the acceptability of scientific knowledge, common to scientists going about the business of doing science. The need for:

- serious attempts to control variables to isolate effects, or the setting up of control experiments;
- reproducibility of results irrespective of the experimenter, time and place;
- as precise a prediction of effects and phenomena as is possible;
- careful estimation of the errors inherent in the experiment so as not to make claims that are unjustified by the information in the data;
- explanations of why things happen in terms of material mechanisms.

Objective

You should be able to comment on the way pupils' learning of science shares common concern with scientists' criteria for the acceptability of scientific knowledge.

Instructions

- Carry out this analysis in conjunction with your work on activity 4.4.
- Look at some activities in a scheme of work that your department may be using.
- Identify the places in the scheme of work where these five criteria may be brought into play as an integral part of the pupils' learning of science.
- If any of the five are not brought into play at any stage in the scheme of work then you should decide how the activities for the pupils might be altered so as to make that incorporation possible.
- Write a brief report on your analysis.
- Discuss your report with your mentor.

7.5 Your Nature of Science Profile

Mentor's Brief

Objective • Student teachers should be aware of their position with respect to major ideas on the way science makes knowledge.

Time • 1 hour for the student teacher working alone and then discussing their profile
- 3 hours for analysis of both Science in the National Curriculum and some departmental schemes of work
- $\frac{1}{2}$ hour discussion of profiles with colleagues

Background

There is some reason to believe that the actions any one of us takes are, to a large extent, determined by beliefs we hold about the appropriateness of such actions: our actions are driven by our philosophies. Few of us have well worked out, unambiguous, philosophies that we can state and interrogate, but it is possible for us to produce a repertoire of responses to specific instances. This questionnaire is intended to help science teachers expose and inspect their own philosophies of science through responding to specific instances.

Instructions

- The student teacher should complete the questionnaire and then read the explanatory notes on the following page. (The questionnaire is taken from Nott & Wellington. 1993)

- The questionnaire can also be given to other members of the science department.
- When the questionnaire has been completed and the student teacher has worked out his or her profile, discuss the results in relation to the science that is being taught to the pupils. This could be a whole department activity.

Discussion points

- Does it matter if all the teachers in a science department have different profiles?
- Are pupils likely to be confused by different philosophies of science presented by different teachers?
- How are student teachers' philosophies of science (and other teachers too) expressed in their presentation of science investigations for pupils?
- Does Science in the National Curriculum have a profile? What is it?
- Which philosophy of science is implicit, or perhaps explicit, in the schemes of work for your department?

7.5   Your Nature of Science Profile

Student Teacher's Brief

This questionnaire is designed to give you some idea of your own philosophy of science. Please read each of the statements carefully. Give each one a number ranging from 'strongly agree' (+5) to 'strongly disagree' (–5) and place it next to the statement — a score of 0 will indicate a balanced view. (For the moment ignore the initials in brackets.)

Questionnaire

1. Results that pupils get from their experiments are as valid as anybody else's. (RP)
2. Science is essentially a masculine subject. (CD)
3. Science facts are what scientists agree they are. (CD, RP)
4. The object of scientific activity is to reveal reality. (IR)
5. Scientists have no idea of the outcome of an experiment before they do it. (ID)
6. Scientific research is economically and politically determined. (CD)
7. Science education should be more about the learning of scientific processes than the learning of scientific facts. (PC)

---

8. The processes of science are divorced from moral and ethical considerations. (CD)
9. The most valuable part of a scientific education is what remains after the facts have been forgotten. (PC)
10. Scientific theories are valid if they work. (IR)
11. Science proceeds by drawing generalizable conclusions (which later become theories) from available data. (ID)
12. There is no such thing as a true scientific theory. (RP, IR)
13. Human emotion plays no part in the creation of scientific knowledge. (CD)
14. Scientific theories describe a real external world which is independent of human perception. (RP, IR)
15. A good solid grounding in basic scientific facts and inherited scientific knowledge is essential before young scientists can go on to make discoveries of their own. (PC)
16. Scientific theories have changed over time simply because experimental techniques have improved. (RP, CD)
17. Scientific method is transferable from one scientific investigation to another. (PC)
18. In practice, choices between competing theories are made purely on the basis of experimental results. (CD, RP)
19. Scientific theories are as much a result of imagination and intuition as inference from experimental results. (ID)
20. Scientific knowledge is different from other kinds of knowledge in that it has higher status. (RP)
21. There are certain physical events in the universe which science can never explain. (RP, IR)
22. Scientific knowledge is morally neutral — only the application of the knowledge is ethically determined. (CD)
23. All scientific experiments and observations are determined by existing theories. (ID)
24. Science is essentially characterized by the methods and processes it uses. (PC)

Producing your profile

You can use your responses, using our scoring system, to work out a profile of your nature of science. Look for the initials in brackets after each statement. Put your score for each question in the appropriate box(es). (Some questions 'score' twice!) Some scores have to have their sign REVERSED (i.e. multiply by (–1) before they can be used. This is indicated by a '–' next to the number, e.g., if your response to statement 1 is –3, then the score in the right-hand column on the RP boxes will be +3.

Table 7.1: Profile of science score boxes

RP statement	score		ID statement	score		CD statement	score		PC statement	score		IR statement	score
1	–		5	–		2	–		7	–		10	–
3	–		11	–		3	–		9	–		21	+
21	–		9	+		6	–		17	–		4	+
12	+		23	+		8	–		24	–		12	+
14	+		total			13	+		15	+		14	+
16	+					16	+		total			total	
18	+					18	+						
20	+					22	+						
total						total							

Transfer the total marks from the columns to the positions on each relevant axis. Join up the 5 marks. This is your profile at the moment.

RELATIVISM   POSITIVISM
−40   −32   −24   −16   −8   RP   8   16   24   32   40

INDUCTIVISM   DEDUCTIVISM
−20   −16   −12   −8   −4   ID   4   8   12   16   20

CONTEXTUALISM   DE-CONTEXTUALISM
−40   −32   −24   −16   −8   CD   8   16   24   32   40

PROCESS DRIVEN   CONTENT DRIVEN
−25   −20   −15   −10   −5   PC   5   10   15   20   25

INSTRUMENTALISM   REALISM
−25   −20   −15   −10   −5   PC   5   10   15   20   25

Figure 7.2:   Five axes for a profile of science

Interpreting your profile

Relativism — Positivism axis
Relativism: The denial that things are true or false solely based on an independent reality. The 'truth' of a theory will depend upon the norms and rationality of the social group considering it as well as the

experimental techniques used to test it. Judgments as to the truth of scientific theories will vary from individual to individual and from one culture to another, i.e. truth is relative not absolute.

Positivism: The belief that scientific knowledge is more valid than other forms of knowledge. The laws and theories generated by experiment are our descriptions of patterns we see in a real external objective world. To the positivist, science is the primary source of truth. Positivism recognizes empirical facts and observable phenomena as the raw materials of science. The scientist's job is to establish the objective relationships between the laws governing the facts and the observables. Positivism rejects enquiry into underlying causes and ultimate origins.

Inductivism — Deductivism axis

Inductivism: The belief that the scientist's job is the interrogation of nature. By observing many particular instances, one is able to infer from the particular to the general and then determine the underlying laws and theories. According to inductivism scientists generalize from a set of observations to a universal law, inductively. Scientific knowledge is built by induction from a secure set of observations.

Deductivism: The belief that scientists proceed by testing ideas produced by the logical consequences of current theories or of their bold imaginative ideas. According to deductivism (or hypothetico-deductivism), scientific reasoning consists of the forming of hypotheses which are not established by the empirical data but may be suggested by them. Science then proceeds by testing the observable consequences of these hypotheses, i.e., observations are directed or led by hypotheses — they are theory laden.

Contextualism — De-contextualism axis

Contextualism: The view that the truth of scientific knowledge and process is inter-dependent with the culture in which the scientist lives and in which it takes place.

De-contextualism: The view that scientific knowledge is independent of its cultural location and sociological structure.

Process — Content axis

Process driven: Science is seen as a characteristic set of identifiable methods/processes. The learning of these is the essential part of science education.

Content driven: Science is characterized by the facts and ideas it has and that the essential part of science is the acquisition and mastery of this body of knowledge.

Instrumentalism — Realism axis

Instrumentalism: Scientific ideas are fine if they work, that is they allow correct predictions to be made. They are instruments that we can use but they say nothing about an independent reality or their own truth.

Realism: The belief that scientific theories are statements about a world that exists in space and time independent of the scientist's perceptions. Correct theories describe things which are really there, independent of the scientists, e.g., atoms.

Chapter 8

Science and People

Aims

It is people who do science and the results of scientific endeavour affect people's lives. The past, the present and the future of science are intimately involved with people: the future of science will be dependent upon our pupils. We may help them to see that they can contribute to that future if we pay attention to the people who developed our scientific knowledge and skills to what they are now. The aims of this chapter are to help student teachers investigate:

- how pupils see science and scientists and to think about what teachers do to promote particular images;
- the contribution a knowledge of the history of science makes to improving science teaching;
- the role of science in society and how can we explore this relationship in the classroom;
- the ways in which the ethical issues that are raised by science might be presented and explored by pupils.

Introduction

A study of the past, present and possible futures for science involves asking questions about the history of science, its social location and the ethical issues that science raises. This is education *about* science rather than education *in* science or science education by *doing* science (Hodson, 1990). It is the part of science education that is most easily lost under the pressure of Attainment Targets, GCSE and 'A' level examinations, report forms and many other routine administrative pressures. It is the part of science education that may not even be attempted because science teachers are, by and large, not historians, sociologists and moral philosophers.

Science teachers do not carry the sole responsibility for the images of science that pupils have. Pupils gain a distorted impression of science from images of science that are presented in everyday life. Television, radio, the cinema and books carry images of scientists and science therefore, even before formal science education begins, young children have some image of scientists and science and activity 8.1 involves researching these images.

Gender differences, as contributors to differentiated outcomes in science education, have been under active investigation since the 1970s. The research findings have contributed to changes in curricular provision. Science in the National Curriculum was, in part, motivated by a perceived need to redress the imbalance between the pupil uptake in different sciences in Years 10, 11 and beyond. It was thought to be a bad thing that many boys could leave school without any formal scientific knowledge of their own bodies or that girls could leave school without any knowledge of the science behind the electromechanical appliances used in daily life. Student teachers are heirs to these changes and need to become aware of their impact on classroom life. Activity 8.2 provides an opportunity to develop pupils' personal responses to science, within topic areas, with links between science in the classroom and daily life.

Individual scientists are historically, socially, economically, politically and geographically located. An awareness of this is very useful to science teachers. The context of science can be exploited in teaching about science by providing pupils with activities that explore science in it's context. This approach goes beyond the simple historical. Inquiring into the application of science in technology is a popular extension activity for pupils. Materials such as *Science and Technology in Society* ('*SATIS*') from the Association for Science Education's and the Heinemann series, *Reading About Science* have had significant uptake in the UK. Activity 8.3 provides student teachers with a structured opportunity to explore the pupil activities in these materials.

The history of science provides an opportunity to introduce a different personal dimension. Our science teaching can benefit from incorporating more on the lives and works of earlier scientists. This aspect is often forgotten or covered in trivial terms by simply associating names with specific ideas. Even a momentary examination of such snippets shows that they are at best simplistic or at worst incorrect, e.g., 'Darwin invented evolution'. In all cases, these scientists were part of a society facing particular problems that brought particular aspects of scientific thinking to the fore. Darwin's achievement was to bring together and make coherent ideas that had been around for some time. So why was this a problem Darwin was prepared to tackle? What was the society he was working in like at the time? What kind of person was he himself? What problems did he face in the development of his idea? The answers to such questions help to set science in a personal context and provide an opportunity for children to realize that science is a human activity. It also breaks the subject barriers that focus pupils attention on differences between subjects. Activities for student teachers in 8.4 are to help them to think more critically about activities for pupils which can build pupils' knowledge of science's past.

'SATIS' materials contain activities that involve questions to which there are moral and ethical dimensions. Activity 8.5 is devoted to these. Such materials are amongst the hardest to use and it takes a skilled, confident teacher, who is sufficiently familiar with the children, to relax their grip on classroom control. Formal debates and discussions, drama and role play are so far removed from standard science teaching that teachers must be confident enough to risk potential failure in adopting them. For this reason the exploration of moral and ethical questions is often left out of classroom activities. Many pupils find these amongst the most interesting aspects of an education *about* science. They are the issues of the day which help shape the future of science.

8.1 Images and Attitudes to Science

Mentor's Brief

Objective • Student teachers should be able to comment on how pupils' images of science might be changed through changing pupils' activities.

Time • 2 hours for student teacher interviews, reflection and writing
• $\frac{1}{2}$ hour discussion with mentor

Background

This activity is designed to provide an opportunity for student teachers to explore children's images and attitudes to science. Research shows that science can be one of the least popular of school subjects (Whitfield, 1979). At the time of change over to compulsory science to Year 11 in the UK, the data for subject choices at A level seem to be showing that a curriculum which forces pupils to study all three sciences for approximately 20 per cent of the curriculum time has not led to an increase in the number of pupils choosing to continue with science post-16.

In particular, the number of girls choosing to study sciences for A level, other than biology, remains disappointingly low. Head (1985) has argued that science is seen as being objective, detached and not concerned with people. The arts, however, are seen to be concerned with emotions, aesthetics and people. Since adolescence is a crucial time when children are seeking to define their identity, subject choice is a statement about the Self. Girls can be put off a subject which seems to be impersonal, unemotive and which does not reflect their values.

When asked to draw a scientist, children predominantly draw the stereotype of a white male in a lab-coat with glasses and wild hair. There is some evidence though that children recognize the limitations of this image and that when asked, 'What do scientists do?' and 'Are real scientists like your drawing?', their answers show a better understanding of science.

Science laboratories themselves can appear to be cold, impersonal environments lacking such creature comforts as carpets, flowers or plants and interesting wall posters. In addition, much of science education is presented through the use of apparatus which sometimes seems deliberately arcane and whose use is restricted solely to the science laboratory, reinforcing the notion that science is a specialist activity undertaken only within institutions rather than giving the impression of science as an everyday activity of great personal relevance.

Instructions

- Brief the student teacher well in advance.
  This activity might be carried out in conjunction with the second part of activity 5.1b.
- Direct the student teacher to pupils in Years 7 and 11.
- Discuss the student teacher's report.

Discussion points

Factors which contribute towards children's impressions of science can be beyond the influence of school: such as the contribution of the media. This discussion should bring out some of the situations and actions in school which contribute towards children's impressions of science and over which the school has control.

- Displaying pupil's work on a regular basis is a routine that teachers can invoke without any major upheaval.
- Having more posters of science in daily life will also have a positive influence.
- Changing the introduction to topics so they draw more heavily on pupils' experiences in daily life.
- Large scale changes in the type of pupil activities, sequencing of activities and learning objectives in schemes of work.
- Every science teacher carries the personal responsibility of promoting science as a worthwhile human endeavour.

8.1 Images and Attitudes to Science

Student Teacher's Brief

Objective

You should be able to comment on how pupils' images of science might be changed through changing pupils' activities.

Instructions

- For this activity, you will need to work with a small group of pupils or alternatively with individual pupils. As a minimum you will need to talk to a boy and girl from Year 7 and Year 11. You should take notes of the answers that the pupils give.
- 'Warm-up' your interviewees by asking them about how their day has gone so far. Explain that the purpose of the activity is to find out what they think scientists' work is and what they think of the science that they do in school. In order to get them to talk freely, you will have to assure them that anything they tell you is confidential.
- After your introduction ask the following:

  Could you please draw a picture of scientist for me?

  Do real scientists look like your picture?

  What do scientists do?

  Can you tell me the names of any scientist that you know?

  Could you write down all the subjects that you do and then sort them into three groups; those you like, those you don't like and those you don't mind.

  You put science in the ....group.

  Can you tell me what it is about science that made you choose that group?

  What activities do you most like doing in science?

  Some pupils think science is boring. What do you think? Why do you think that?

  What would make science more interesting for you?

- Go into a room used for teaching English and make a few notes on the appearance of the room.

  How is it furnished?

  Are there recent posters on the wall?

  Is children's work displayed?

  Is there any specialist apparatus and what impression of the subject does it give?

- Now go to a typical science laboratory and ask the same questions. What impression do you get from any apparatus or specimens that might be out or on show in display cabinets?
- Try and summarize your overall impressions of the contrast between the two.
- Write a brief report on your findings. Consider the following in your report:

  What image do pupils have of science?

  What attitudes do pupils have to science?

  Which school experiences are possibly responsible for forming their impressions?

> How might school science activities be changed so as to put a more human face on science?

8.2   Promoting a More Personal Response

Mentor's Brief

Objective • The student teacher should construct a display that develops the theme of science in everyday life for some topic taken from a scheme of work, and use it in teaching the topic.

Time • 3–4 hours student teacher preparation
• $\frac{1}{2}$ hour discussion with mentor

Background

Young children are naturally very concerned with themselves and their own personal identity and enjoy that element of the personal and subjective. The personal element is an aspect student teachers often overlook initially, seeing their task as one of delivering the teaching and learning of the concepts in the department's scheme of work. This activity seeks to explore how we can encourage the personal response in education *about* science by relating science to features of pupils' daily lives.

Instructions

• Identify a topic that might be imminent in the programme of study for pupils in classes that the student teacher will be working with.
• Direct the student teacher to the activity notes.
• Discuss progress on compiling the display with the student teacher.
• Arrange for the lesson in which the display will be team taught.
• Arrange for feedback to the student teacher on the effectiveness of the activity.
• Discuss the use of such activities, and alternative activities, with the student teacher.

Discussion points

• The display helps to bring the everyday world into the science lesson.
• The invitation to open ended writing makes the start of a topic more approachable as there are no 'right' answers.

- Pupils, as is everyone, are more at ease with the familiar and this builds confidence to proceed.
- Bringing the real world into the classroom will probably be more effective than using photographs, cartoons, text and video clips. So, for example, real spectacles, real bottles and glasses and real tanks of water would be better.
- Field-trips, hospital, factory and workshop visits as well illustrated talks by speakers all help to bring the world into the classroom. Local SATRO representatives will be able to help put you in touch with local industry. The contact address for the National SATRO co-ordinator is in this book, Appendix 2 (see p. 211).

8.2 Promoting a More Personal Response

Student Teacher's Brief

Objective

You should construct a display that develops the theme of science in everyday life for some topic taken from a scheme of work and use it in your teaching.

Instructions

- Discuss with your mentor a suitable topic from the programme of study in your school, e.g., refraction.
- Think carefully about how the science involved enables you to explain events in everyday life. Write out what the everyday events are, e.g., seeing differently through spectacles; looking at objects through other transparent objects, like bottles and glasses; looking at the bottom of a swimming pool etc.
- Collect documentation of those events in everyday life. You might collect photographs, newspaper articles, cartoons, video-clips.
- Compile your documentation into a display that can be used as a pupil activity to start the topic.
- Think about how the display is presented to the pupils and what they will be asked to do. You might:
    - ask them to write an open ended piece about what they notice in the montage. This could take different forms poems, letters, newspaper articles;
    - invite them to make guesses about the science that is common to the elements in the display. This could be a written task;
    - provide them with a series of structured questions;

> group questions and frame them so that they form a type of comprehension exercise that goes from reporting what is in the montage to explaining how things happen.
>
> - Consider what the next activity for the pupils might be in terms of focusing their attention more carefully on the phenomenon involved. Write out a brief scheme of work (topics and activities) for the next four lessons that follow on from the display introduction.
> - Trial your activities in a team-teaching situation.
> - Devise amendments in the light of pupil responses.
> - Now consider these questions for discussion with your mentor:
>   How might the work with the display help pupils to have a more personal response to science?
>   What might be more effective than a display?
>   How else could you link science to daily life?

8.3   Science And Technology In Society: The SATIS Materials

Mentor's Brief

Objective • Student teachers should be able to identify a variety of different pupil activities involved in SATIS-type work.

Time • 1 hour student teacher review of SATIS materials
 • 15 minutes discussion with mentor

Background

The application of science is intimately bound up with technology, and technology changes the way people live their lives. Science and technology are not the same thing but many people have difficulty in distinguishing between the two. A crucial distinction lies in the fact that science has theories that enable it to consider the question, 'Why does it happen?' Technology as practised by many societies was, and is still, nothing more than a 'trial and error' technology. Societies two thousand years ago in Africa, and even as recently as two hundred years ago in Britain, may have known how to make steel but they had no conception of why the process worked and therefore no idea of how to improve the process, other than by tinkering. Successful scientific theories enable predictions to be made which can be tested against experimental evidence and have stood the test of time.

The traditional approach to science teaching has tended to place applications as an after-thought and treated technology as being a bolt-on extra. There have been efforts to strengthen the links in secondary science education through resource materials such as those published by Hobsons in their series of Science Plus: *Biology Plus*, *Chemistry Plus* and *Physics Plus*. However the 'Plus' does not challenge the myth that first there is science and then there is its application, thus totally ignoring the other direction of flow in this two-way street where technology provides science with the phenomena it might investigate together with the social setting in which such issues are seen as being worthy of research.

The fact remains that technology is the most visible, pervasive and intrusive aspect to scientific development and change. Pupils are daily confronted with technology in a way they are not confronted with science. *Salters Science*, for example, takes as its starting points 'Food', 'Clothing', 'Warmth', 'Drink' and 'Buildings'. These topic titles acknowledge that the issues of technology, its uses and abuses, are far more pressing in pupils' minds than the question of 'Why does it happen?'

Instructions

- Direct the student teacher to survey SATIS materials and then to report back.
- Discuss the student teacher's report.

Discussion points

The SATIS materials include the following generic activities:

questionnaires where pupils must check to agree/disagree/don't know;
debates as role plays;
comprehension exercises;
data analysis exercises;
small group discussions;
suggested experiments.

It is useful to highlight this point about generic activities in pointing to how the techniques can be adapted to other content material.

8.3 Science And Technology In Society: The SATIS Materials

Student Teacher's Brief

Objective

You should be able to identify a variety of different pupil activities in SATIS-type work.

Instructions

- Collect a set of SATIS materials for one age group.
- Quickly scan the materials to see what they contain and what the format is.
- Return to work through them systematically. Don't read the materials, rather, look for
  — patterns in the ways in which they locate science and technology in a social context.
  — the different types of pupil activity that re-occur.
- Keep notes as you work. A chart or table might be useful.
- Report back to your mentor.

8.4 Incorporating Historical Material

Mentor's Brief

Objective • Student teachers should be able to construct worksheets that make use of historical material and to trial them with groups of pupils.

Time • 3–4 hours student teacher preparation
• ¹/₂ hour discussion with history teacher

Background

There are different approaches to the study of history. In science the most popular approach is that of 'the great man'. The 'great man' view of history is underlined by the nomenclature of units associated with their work. This particular approach to history is not helpful in science education. Firstly, it does not accurately model the historical process itself, in which the bit-part players are just as important as the hero of the piece. Secondly, the focus on biography gives rise to anecdote, not always accurate, and often misleading, in terms of how knowledge is advanced. Thirdly, the conceptual changes for which the 'hero' was responsible are actually trivialized in paying no attention, or caustically dismissing, what went before. More pressing, from the point of view of science education, the 'great man' approach can alienate rather than encourage: 'There were so few who were successful, how can I possibly be like them?'

An alternative is to focus on the explanation of some natural phenomenon that pupils have been studying. The question of what the pupils think about that phenomenon should have already been raised — they may be unclear in their own ideas — so it is encouraging for pupils to learn that they are not alone: other people thought as they do. This then re-directs attention onto ideas and the evidence that led to those ideas being changed, and some of the changes of the past are echoed in the pupils of today. Pupils can be encouraged through knowing that if others have started from the same position and moved forwards, so can they.

The key advantage to this approach, from the point of view of constructing a scheme of work, is that history has a natural place in helping pupils change their ideas. It does not have to be bolted on. Education *in* science can be combined with education *about* science.

The student teacher will need access to illustrated books that contain information on the history of science. The ASE in conjunction with the British Society for the History of Science have published a *Directory of Resources*. The address is given in Appendix 2 (see p. 211).

Instructions

- Direct the student teacher to the activity.
- Discuss the student teacher's worksheets after he or she has visited the history department.

8.4 Incorporating Historical Material

Student Teacher's Brief

Lip-service has long been paid to the notion that a complete science education is one that incorporates some elements of the history of science. The problem is how to do this and when to do this. A possible place in a scheme of work is after pupils have explored some natural phenomenon and produced their own ideas as to what is happening and why. Being familiar with the phenomenon, and puzzled by it, they may be more interested in the history of how it is that we now think what we do.

Objective

You should be able to construct worksheets that make use of historical material and trial them with groups of pupils.

Instructions

- Discuss a suitable topic from the programme of study in your school with your mentor.

- You will need access to books that deal with the history of science and are well illustrated. Find out the following:

  What did the scientist most associated with this topic think?

  How did the scientist come to this opinion?

  What was the key evidence?

  What did people think about the phenomenon beforehand?

  Why did they think that?

  (Pupils might be encouraged to recognize elements of their own ideas in the thoughts of people from the past. Their ideas can be rendered less naïve, and thereby less alienating to the purpose of learning science, if they can see they are not alone)

  What was life like at that time in that place?

  How had this phenomenon come to attention and why was it in need of exploration and explanation?

  How had your chosen scientist become involved?

  What biographical data can you find out about the scientist?

- Find pictures related to the scientist's life and times.
- Now put together **two** worksheets. Be imaginative in your compilation.

  The first should be on the development of the scientific ideas.

  The second should focus on the life and times of the scientist.

- For each of the above you will need to do the following.

  Write out your own text and add illustrations.

  It should not be any more than one page of A4.

  Write comprehension questions to go with each of the texts and illustrations.

  Nine questions are probably enough.

  Structure the questions.

  The first three questions should ask for information that can be obtained by copying from the text directly or describing an illustration.

  The fourth to sixth questions should require the pupils to combine or compare information in the text or illustrations.

  The last three questions should ask the pupils for their opinions about issues that are related but not explicitly in the text.

- Take your comprehension worksheets to a history teacher in the school. Ask them for their opinion and advice on your efforts.
- Trial your worksheets with pupils.
- Discuss the results with your mentor.

8.5   Ethical and Moral Issues

Mentor's Brief

Objective • Student teachers should be able to report on how moral and ethical issues might be incorporated into a revised scheme of work.

Time • 3 hours for student teacher preparation tasks
 • $\frac{1}{2}$ hour discussion with drama teacher

Background

The introduction of moral and ethical issues can be a very motivating feature of science education for young people. Student teachers need a great deal of confidence and some help in devising appropriate strategies for such pupil activities. The debate format is undoubtedly easier to handle than the more open-ended drama. Both might be best placed at the end of a term and perhaps towards the end of a student teacher's training period. This work should be part of the revision of a scheme of work that is discussed in section 4.5.

Instructions

 • Direct the student teacher to this activity as part of the work on activity 4.5.

8.5   Ethical and Moral Issues

Student Teacher's Brief

Science throws up ethical and moral questions which are of great interest to young people who want to know how they should behave and how other people are likely to behave in given situations. Science teachers avoid these because they are rarely, if ever, part of a syllabus for examination and teachers themselves do not have a repertoire of skills for providing suitable pupil activities.

Objective

You should be able to report on how moral and ethical issues might be incorporated into a revised scheme of work.

Instructions

The following are SATIS 14-to-16 activities that involve debate or public inquiry. They offer one way of handling moral or ethical issue with a class:

409 Dam problems
502 The coal mine project
503 Paying for the National Health
602 The limestone quarry
608 Should we build a fall-out shelter?
1002 Quintonal: an industrial hazard
1003 A big bang.

You should do the following:

- Review the SATIS activities listed above.
- Decide how they work.
  What are their mechanisms in terms of pupil activities?
- Devise a debate activity that can be included in the scheme of work for the topic you are revising in conjunction with your work in section 4.5
- Discuss your debate outline with your mentor.

Drama can provide a way of exploring moral and ethical issues with a class. You should do the following:

- Discuss with a drama teacher in your school how they go about structuring pupils' activities for the workshop development of a play. Find out the following.
  What are good opening activities?
  How this is followed up?
  How is the development of the play organized by the teacher?
  How are pupils' roles and the plot line developed?
  Do the pupils do any writing?
  What record is kept of the pupils' work?

Chapter 9

Progression in Pupils' Ideas

Aims

The aims of this chapter are to:

- make student teachers aware of the concepts that pupils of differing age and ability hold about some common natural phenomena;
- offer student teachers an explanation of that diversity in terms of a model of cognitive development;
- characterize the main features of the model and the stages of cognitive development that the model describes;
- introduce the idea of assessing the cognitive demand made by science concepts, and of choosing levels of concepts to suit pupils of varying age and ability;
- start student teachers thinking about ways of encouraging cognitive growth in their pupils, especially through the use of well-designed cognitive conflict activities.

Introduction

Pupils can make progress through the science curriculum in a number of ways:

- from one topic to another (from respiration to photosynthesis);
- from one context to another (from respiration in mammals, through respiration in insects, to respiration in plants);
- in the complexity of the concepts they deal with (from respiration as 'oxygen plus sugar produces carbon dioxide and warmth' to the 'cellular chemistry of respiration').

This chapter is concerned with the last of these. It is based on the idea that children's ability to process information, their thinking ability, develops slowly with experience and interaction, and that the information-processing capability of a particular child will set limits on the complexity of concepts that the child can cope with. Such a view has serious implications for science education.

We have operations in the working of our minds, or ways of thinking, which enable us to construct knowledge. Jean Piaget and his co-workers in Geneva found that these cognitive operations develop progressively and sequentially. This development is not just a matter of becoming faster or more full of knowledge: there are qualitative changes in the way that children process new information as they develop cognitively. Stages of cognitive development were identified by Piaget and labelled as sensori-motor, pre-operational, concrete and formal operational.

In secondary science education we generally require pupils to use concrete and formal operations. Concrete operations are mental operations on concrete variables, that is variables which can be directly perceived, such as length, weight, colour or shape. Formal operations are concerned with variables that are derived, second order; such as density, pressure or oxidation number. Formal operations are needed to use abstract models, such as kinetic theory or theoretical models of the atom or cell, to make predictions about the effect of changes in model parameters on the macro properties of materials or organisms. For more detail and examples of science concepts available at each stage of cognitive development, see *Towards a Science of Science Teaching* (Shayer & Adey, 1981).

There is some controversy as to whether 'concrete operational' and 'formal operational' may properly be used as descriptions of individual children. Does concrete operational behaviour in one context signify a general characteristic of the child, that is will the same child use concrete operations in a different, more familiar, context? In this chapter, a strong Piagetian line is taken in recognizing that pupils' stages of cognitive development will limit the responses they can make to a problem. But recognition is also given to the fact that however intellectually powerful people may be, they cannot solve a problem unless they have the necessary background knowledge. Both knowledge and processing ability are necessary for academic achievement.

During their first weeks in school, student teachers need to become aware of the fact that pupils have a range of ideas about different natural phenomena. In activity 9.1, student teachers are directed to explore the ideas individual pupils hold. The activity involves talking to pupils and recording their views. It is essentially a data collection activity. The data can then be used for activity 9.2, in which student teachers are invited to find patterns in the pupils' ideas. Initially this sifting and sorting relies on the student teachers' intuitive categories. Later in the activity, the student teachers are introduced to descriptions of Piagetian stages and invited to use these to categorize pupils' ideas collected in 9.1. Activity 9.3 develops student teachers' familiarity with the Piagetian stages through asking them to apply the descriptions of different stages to analyse objectives appropriate to learning science. The analysis can be extended to Science in the National Curriculum. Some grasp of progression in the levels of the attainment targets can be achieved from this activity.

One of the tenets of the Piagetian model of cognitive development is that children progress through cognitive action. Children need to have experiences that make them think. Science teachers must therefore find activities for pupils that require thinking. The choice of activity and the sequencing of activities play an important part in providing pupils with the cognitive conflict that aids their cognitive development. Activity 9.4 allows student teachers to consider how their lesson planning and schemes of work in science might accelerate pupils' cognitive development.

Progression and differentiation are the obverse and reverse of the same coin. Student teachers are directed to consider the implications of different rates of progression amongst pupils. In any one class there will always be a spread of pupils' thinking. That spread is obviously greater in mixed performance or unstreamed classes. Teachers need strategies to help pupils at different stages of progress. In activity 9.5 student teachers are directed to consider the issue of differentiation.

9.1 Children's Ideas about Natural Phenomena

Mentor's Brief

Objective • Student teachers should be able to report on the range of pupils' ideas on selected natural phenomena.

Time • 2 hours to interview a range of pupils on different phenomena
 • $\frac{1}{2}$ hour discussion with mentor

Background

Student teachers often find it difficult to come to terms with the way in which many pupils seem to fail to understand apparently basic concepts in science. They tend to assume understanding has been achieved just because the material has been carefully explained, a practical has been done, and the pupils have seemed to attend and nod sagely. This activity is intended to give the student teacher first-hand experience of the types of concepts which children form.

Instructions

• Select Year 8 or 9 pupils for the student teacher to interview for their ideas on natural phenomena. (Year 9 is best in a mixed ability school for producing a suitable range of different ideas from the pupils. Do not use Year 7 pupils as it is too easy for student teachers to write off their misconceptions 'because they have not been taught it yet'. To avoid pupils' ideas being rationalized as idiosyncratic, do not choose pupils who are either exceptionally bright or who have serious learning difficulties. The student teacher should have the opportunity to see that some misconceptions are common even with average pupils.)

- Discuss with the student teacher the topic on which they will collect data. Suggested questions on three topics are in the student teachers' notes:

    The Earth in space
    Current electricity
    Solutions

- Guide the student teacher with the advice that each interview should last about 15 minutes.
- Discuss the student teacher's experiences after the interviews.

Discussion points

It is important to impress upon the student teacher that what might appear at first sight to be a rather shocking level of misconceptions amongst pupils is in fact not unusual. This is not to say that we should be content with it, but to highlight a very common phenomenon and so be better prepared to deal with it.

9.1   Children's Ideas about Natural Phenomena

Student Teacher's Brief

Although you can get some idea of what pupils think about different science concepts by looking at their written work, the best way to probe their understanding is by talking to them. Pupils have a range of ideas, many of which can be quite sophisticated in complexity. Many of their ideas are not the same as those of scientists. Teaching science involves working with pupils' ideas and helping pupils to change their minds.

Objective

You should be able to report on the range of pupils' ideas on selected natural phenomena.

Instructions

You must have a pencil and paper for the pupil to draw on. You might find it useful to tape the interviews. For the electricity topic, a cell, some connecting wires and a couple of bulbs would be useful but not essential. For the work on solutions, a glass of water and some salt or sugar will be handy.

- Your mentor will select some pupils for you to talk with.
- Three topics are suggested below. Decide with your mentor

---

which topic you wish to investigate, and interview all of the pupils on the same topic. If you have plenty of time, you could then do a second topic.

- Below are some notes on possible questions for three topic areas. Read the notes.
- Check with the class teachers that you can talk with their pupils.
- Tell the pupils that you are not assessing them, just trying to find out more about what pupils think.
- In every case, start off with some easy questions, and gradually probe more deeply, but if the pupil is obviously lost, do not press for high level answers.

  Take your time, and allow the pupil plenty of time to answer, letting the pupil talk around the topic. Provide the minimum amount of help needed to move the interview on.

  Vary your questioning according to the responses the pupils makes.

  Your aim is to find out as much as possible about what they think.

- Keep a record of pupils' ideas by writing notes as they talk. Encourage them to make drawings. Collect the drawings and label them with their names.
- Discuss how the interviews went with your mentor.
- Keep your notes for analysis in activity 9.2.

Notes on possible questions for three topic areas

The Earth in space

What sort of shape do you think the Earth is?

Have you heard people say that the Earth is round? Do you think they mean like a football, or flat like a disc (record)?

Draw what you think the Earth is like.

Draw some people standing on the Earth.

Can you draw another person standing on the other side of the Earth (in Australia)?

Draw some clouds with rain falling on the people.

Why don't the people fall off?

What do you think gravity is? Where does it come from?

Solutions

What happens if you put a little salt in water and stir it? How does this happen?

Is the salt still there?

In what way is the water similar or different from how it was to start with?

In what ways is the salt similar or different to how it was before?
Does the solution weigh more, less, or the same as the water before
   the salt was added?
If I went on adding more and more salt, what would happen?
What would happen to the weight of the water?
If I did it in a measuring cylinder, would the level of water rise?

Probe for some sort of explanation in terms of 'particles' of salt and
particles of water. If appropriate, seek deeper understanding in terms
of sodium and chloride ions.

Current electricity

Can you make this bulb light, using this battery and wires? (in
   practice or as a drawing)
What makes the bulb light?
Where does the electricity come from?
What happens to the electric current when it goes through the bulb?
Show me how it travels from the battery to the bulb. Put arrows
   on the wires in your drawing to show the direction it flows.

At this point you may need to make some corrections to ensure that
they have a complete circuit.

Is there the same amount of current all around the circuit, or is there
less in some places than others? Why is this? How could you test
this?

If all of this has been easy, draw or make a circuit like this:

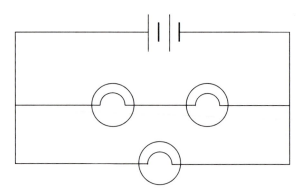

Figure 9.1:   An electrical circuit suitable for discussion with pupils

Ask questions about current in each part, about energy transfer in the bulbs or about what happens if you unscrew each bulb in turn.

More probing questions include:

If the same current returns to the battery as leaves it, what is transferred from the battery to the bulbs? How?

9.2a   Patterns in Children's Ideas about Natural Phenomena

Mentor's Brief

Objective   • Student teachers should be able to examine children's ideas to see if there is patterning and consistency.

Time   • 2 hours for the student teacher to interpret their data, read the notes, make comparisons and write a brief report
   • $\frac{1}{2}$ hour discussion with mentor

Background

Questions like those in activity 9.1 have been asked of pupils by researchers in many schools (see Driver, *et al*, 1994). Student teachers need to be aware that the misconceptions revealed in the interviews are not peculiar to your school or to this particular group of pupils. Since they are widespread it is likely that they are systematic. Key determining factors arise from the complexity of the concepts and from the limitations in pupils' abilities to process such concepts. Later activities in this chapter will explore ways of describing this complexity and suggest what might be done to increase pupils' processing ability.

Instructions

   • Direct the student teacher to the activity which involves sifting and sorting the data obtained from activity 9.1. (Note that the categories in the table for different age cohorts are taken from research findings. The percentages in the table were taken from survey data collected on the distribution of Piagetian stages of cognitive processing.)
   • Discuss the student teacher's report.

Discussion points

   • Student teachers should get a feeling for the way in which pupils' ideas are not random but are systematic. The fact that they are systematic means that it is possible for teachers to find ways of helping pupils change their minds given the constraints of the stage of cognitive processing of the pupils.

- Experimental error is a problem with small samples of pupils especially if the sample itself is not representative of the distribution of Piagetian stages across a same-age cohort.

9.2a Patterns in Children's Ideas about Natural Phenomena

Student Teacher's Brief

Objective

You should be able to examine children's ideas to see if there is patterning and consistency.

Instructions

Complete these first two steps before you read further instructions below:

- Sift and sort the pupils' responses to your interviews in activity 9.1, with a view to finding regularity and patterns in their ideas.
- Group ideas that are similar together. In what ways are they similar?
  Try to write out a characterization for each of the groups.
- Now study the table below on patterning in children's ideas about natural phenomena.
- Compare your grouping with those in the table in the notes below.
- Look at the expected percentages across groups as displayed in the table.
- Review the frequencies in the patterns in your pupils' responses.
- Write up your findings.
- Discuss your report with your mentor.

Notes on patterns in children's ideas

Below are some percentages, derived by interpolation from survey data on children's stages of cognitive development, for what one might expect of pupils at different ages who give different responses to interviews in the three topic areas of activity 9.1.

Table 9.1: *Theory generated expected percentages of pupils with different responses to three topic areas*

Answer type	approximate % of pupils at three ages giving that answer type		
	9+	11+	13+
The Earth in space			
The Earth is flat like a disc. An absolute idea of down. People live inside spherical Earth, or on a flat surface of a hemisphere.	10	5	–
People live all over the surface of the Earth, but drawing shows them all the same way up relative to the page	40	30	35
People on surface of Earth, feet all towards the centre. Idea of 'down' relative to surface or centre of Earth.	45	55	60
Current electricity			
Only one wire needed.	10	5	–
Two wires, current comes down both from cell to bulb.	40	30	25
Current circulates, gets less as it goes around.	45	55	60
Current remains constant.	5	10	15
Solutions			
Salt 'disappears', water gets no heavier.	10	5	–
Salt mixes with water, which gets heavier, but no change in volume. Salt is still there but may not be recoverable.	40	30	25
The process is reversible, salt and water can be recovered.	45	55	60
Some sort of explanation in terms of particles of salt and particles of water mixing.	5	10	15

9.2b   Stages in Cognitive Progression

Mentor's Brief

Objective • Student teachers should be able to use their knowledge of Piagetian stages of cognitive progression to categorize pupils' ideas on natural phenomena.

Time • 2 hours for the student teacher to read the notes, interpret the data and write a brief report
• $\frac{1}{2}$ hour discussion with mentor

Background

Piagetian stage theory provides science teachers with an explanation for the differences in performance by pupils, both as the pupils get older, in progression, and comparing pupils of the same age in differentiated performances. It therefore has the potential to provide guidance on the selection of pupil activities and the grading of tasks in sequences of increasing demand. This is also valuable for interpreting Science in the National Curriculum and translating curriculum documents into graded schemes of work.

Instructions

- Direct the student teacher to the reading, interpretation and report writing activity.
- Supplementary reading is Shayer, M. and Adey, P., (1981).
- Discuss the written report with the student teacher.

Discussion points

- The Piagetian model helps to reduce the complexity of the topic dependence of pupils' ideas. Teachers can apply the same sequence of stages in progression when planning for progression and differentiation in all topic areas.
- Teachers can plan for progression and differentiation within any topic area given sufficient knowledge of the pupil population and the cognitive demand of the topic.
- Using research into children's ideas, the match between curriculum and performance can be improved. Curriculum development can be more systematic.

9.2b   Stages in Cognitive Progression

Student Teacher's Brief

Objective

You should be able to use their knowledge of Piagetian stages of cognitive progression to categorize pupils' ideas on natural phenomena.

Instructions

- Read through the notes on cognitive progression below.
- Use the specimen analysis below to interpret the patterns you found in activity 9.2a.
- Write a brief report on your interpretation.
- Discuss the report with your mentor.

Notes on stages in cognitive progression

The answers which pupils gave in your interview in activity 9.1 are a product of:

---

what they have been taught, and;

what sense they have made of their lessons and do make of your questions.

The sense pupils make of things depends on their ability to process information, and this is a function both of what they know already, and of their thinking skills. The development of their thinking skills takes place through a series of 'stages' each building on the former but being qualitatively different from it.

The main stages of cognitive development described by the Swiss psychologist Jean Piaget are Sensori-motor, Preoperational, Concrete operational, and Formal operational. The great majority of pupils in secondary schools will have reached the concrete or formal stages. What follows is a general account of the different thinking characteristic of the stages.

Pre-operational (1)

Pre-operational pupils offer inconsistent observations. They tend to treat each observation separately and do not group objects consistently in classes but instead change the class of an object according to the immediate circumstances. Their so-called egocentric thought leaves them unable to see things from another's point of view or to generalize. There is a tendency to impute will into inanimate objects. The pre-operational thinker does not conserve any quantities, i.e., they may report that volume, mass, or length have changed when an object is moved or deformed.

Early concrete operations (2A)

At the early concrete stage, children can mentally place objects or observations into groups. They can perceive and use simple two-variable causal relationships in linguistic form: 'When this goes up, that goes down, so this causes that'. Early concrete thinkers can order a series of objects, have a sense of number and therefore can make some sense of measurement. Early concrete thinkers are at the threshold of what is required by a scientific approach to the world. Their ability to conserve some quantities through transformations and their increasing skill in measurement opens up a world of empirical work.

Mature concrete operations (2B)

Mature concrete operators can mentally model crossed categories. For instance, with floating and sinking objects they can see that there are light sinkers and heavy floaters as well as heavy sinkers and light floaters. However, they cannot provide any explanation for such observations which requires imagined or abstract concepts (such as density). Reasoning is reversible: if acids make litmus go red, then anything which makes litmus go red is an acid. Despite the fact that they conserve mass, they have difficulty with displaced volume: they will not equate the rise in volume of a liquid to the volume of a solid which sinks into it. Because the mature concrete operator cannot imagine all of the possible variables in a situation, they will not be able to design an efficient experiment in which all variables are well controlled. Mature concrete operators will be able to follow detailed step-by-step instructions for some practical activity, but may have no overview of what it is all about.

Early formal operations (3A)
Formal operations are mental operations on imagined entities. The formal operational pupil is able to hold a number of variables in mind at once and see how they may be related to one another. Early formal operations offer the beginning of explanatory thinking, so particle models of matter can be used and the theoretical concept of density, if offered, can be used as an explanation for floating and sinking.

Mature formal operations (3B)
Flexible and fluent use of theoretical models and the ability to generate hypotheses and design experiments to test them is the hall mark of the professional scientist. They are also characteristics of the mature formal operational thinker.

A specimen analysis of children's ideas by Piagetian stage

Table 9.2: *A possible Piagetian analysis of pupils' ideas on three topic areas*

Stage	The Earth in space	Current Electricity	Solutions
1	Earth is flat like a disc, an absolute idea of down.	Only one wire needed	Salt 'disappears', water gets no heavier.
2A	People live all over the surface of the Earth, drawings show them all same way up.	Two wires, current comes down both from cell to bulb.	Salt mixes with water which gets heavier, but no change in volume. Salt is still there, but may not be recoverable.
2B	People on surface of the Earth, feet all towards centre.	Current circulates, gets less as it goes around.	The process is reversible, salt and water can be recovered.
3	Idea of down relative to centre of the Earth.	Current remains constant.	Explanation in terms of particles of salt and water mixing.

9.3 Analysing for Cognitive Demand

Mentor's Brief

Objective • Student teachers should be able to use their knowledge of progression in cognitive processing to analyse the level of cognitive demand in lessons and in Science in the National Curriculum.

Time • 6 hours for the student teacher in reading, analysis and report writing
• 1 hour discussion with mentor

Background

There are two activities in this section. In the first the student teacher analyses the plan of a lesson already taught so as to determine what cognitive demand it made. The second activity involves scrutinizing the national curriculum for progression in cognitive demand.

In discussing these activities with the student teacher, it would be useful to have available either or both of *Towards a Science of Science Teaching* (TSST) or the *Thinking Science INSET pack*. TSST has a 'Curriculum Analysis Taxonomy' which offers a comprehensive, if rather complex, method of analysing objectives for level of demand, and the INSET pack includes a complete analysis of the 1991 science national curriculum (even though this has been superseded, the principle of curriculum analysis remains unchanged).

Instructions

• Direct the student teacher to the activity.
• Discuss the student teacher's written reports.

Discussion points

At this stage of the student teacher's development it is enough for these activities to be used to point to what many experienced science teachers know tacitly and intuitively.

• Description is easier than explanation.
• Pupils develop measuring skills alongside their conceptualization of variables.
• Numerical and correlational work are easier for pupils if they are routinized and even ritualized, e.g., calculating strengths of solutions; ratios of F1 hybrids, and currents in circuits by substitution in untransposed equations.

These observations can be accounted for using Piagetian stages of development in pupils' thinking. For example, algebraic work will only make sense to formal operational thinkers. Number work is within the potential skills of late concrete thinkers. Description is easier than explanation because it makes lower conceptual demands. Generally what one thinks depends upon how one thinks.

9.3a Analysing Lessons

Student Teacher's Brief

Tasks which demand formal operational thinking will be difficult for many pupils in Years 7–11 not just because of language demands (see Chapter 6) or unfamiliarity, but because they require a higher level of thinking than the learners have available. You can use this idea in lesson planning, both to ensure that thinking demands are realistic for a particular class, and also to provide differentiation within a lesson for pupils of different abilities.

Objective

You should be able to use your knowledge of progression in the development of pupils' thinking to analyse lessons for cognitive difficulty.

Instructions

- Review ideas on curriculum analysis by reading Shayer and Adey, (1981).
- Look at a lesson plan you have written for a Year 9 or 10 class Chapters 8 and 9.
- Consider in detail the specific learning objectives and the particular learning experiences of the lesson.
    - What concepts do you want pupils to develop?
    - What sort of mental construction do you expect them to undertake?
    - How will the learning experiences help them to construct the target concepts?
    - What level of processing will pupils require for each part of the lesson: early or late concrete, or formal operations.
- Write a brief report on your analysis.
- Discuss your report with your mentor.

9.3b   Cognitive Demand in Science in the National Curriculum

Student Teacher's Brief

Objective

You should be able to use your knowledge of progression in the development of pupils' thinking to analyse Science in the National Curriculum for cognitive difficulty.

Instructions

- Select an attainment target in Science in the National Curriculum dealing with a subject with which you are familiar.
- Starting at the first level of development and working through to level 10, try to estimate the level of thinking (from pre-operational through to late formal operations) that each makes.
- At which level of development do you estimate formal operational thinking to be required?
- Write a brief report on your findings.
- Discuss your report with your mentor.

9.4   Promoting Cognitive Development

Mentor's Brief

Objective   • Student teachers should be able to devise pupil activities that might promote cognitive development

Time   • 3 hours for the student teacher to devise, teach, evaluate and report
   • $\frac{1}{2}$ hour for discussion with mentor

Background

Much of science teaching is normally concerned with instruction: providing pupils with knowledge, cognitive and manipulative skills. The effectiveness of instruction is limited by pupils' ability to process information. We know

now that it is also possible to work directly on this processing ability, to improve the use that pupils make of the instruction they receive. This is known as intervention, because it intervenes in pupils' 'natural' progress in cognitive development and raises their levels of thinking. One of the key elements in this method is cognitive conflict — the setting of problems which cause pupils to stretch their thinking powers. (For more detail of the methods and results, see Adey and Shayer, 1994; Adey, Shayer and Yates, 1989). Although you cannot be expected to go into much detail of cognitive acceleration with student teachers, they should at least be aware of its existence and potential, and have met the idea of cognitive conflict.

Instructions

- Direct the student teacher to the reading on cognitive conflict.
- Discuss the reading and direct the student teacher to devise an activity which provides pupils with conflict. This should be worked into a lesson plan.
- Arrange to team-teach as a participant observer with the student teacher, teaching to their lesson plan.
- Debrief the student teacher and suggest future follow up work of a similar nature.

Discussion points

- Maintaining cognitive conflict is challenging, but not impossibly difficult, and is a professional skill which may take years to develop.
- Doing it for pupils of a wide range of abilities is even more difficult, but it is possible.

9.4 Promoting Cognitive Development

Student Teacher's Brief

Objective

You should be able to devise pupil activities that might promote cognitive development.

Instructions

- Read the notes on cognitive conflict below.
- Discuss the notes with your mentor.

- Devise an activity (or a number of activities) in your own science subject which will generate cognitive conflict. Incorporate these into lesson plans for lessons you will be teaching in the near future.
- Discuss your lesson plans with other science teachers and with your mentor.
  Revise the lesson plans in the light of their comments.
- Team-teach the activity with your mentor.
- Evaluate the pupil activity as you proceed.
  How do the pupils react?
  Do you find this kind of teaching hard work?
  Do they find it hard work?
  How will you modify the activity for future use?
- De-brief with your mentor.

Notes on cognitive conflict

One of the elements of successful cognitive stimulation is called cognitive conflict. This means presenting pupils with an experience which they find surprising, or difficult to understand, which does not fit with their previous understanding and which demands a different way of thinking. Here is an outline of one example:

A teacher takes his class through an activity on rates of reaction, in which the same amount of marble chips is added to a series of test tubes each containing the same volume of hydrochloric acid of the same concentration. Each test tube is at a different temperature and the time taken for the marble chips to dissolve is measured. From this a concrete, two-variable, relationship is established: the higher the temperature the faster the reaction. The teacher asks the pupils to predict how long the reaction would take at other temperatures, which have not been tried, and thus establishes that the relationship can be used to make predictions.

Now he introduces a new experiment, measuring the rate of production of carbon dioxide as yeast ferments. Again a range of temperatures is tried, from just below room temperature to about 30°C. Again it is shown that at higher temperatures the reaction is faster. Again predictions are asked for: what will the rate be like at 40°C and at 50°C? This time pupils are asked to test their predictions — and of course the predictions fail! The simple model they have been using does not work, and they are forced to re-assess the relationship and seek an explanation for the new result.

Note that the pupils have been carefully prepared, they know what the experiment is about, they have been led to expect that they can predict what will happen. Their confusion does not arise because of the difficulty of the concepts, nor because of language difficulties.

9.5 Differentiation

Mentor's Brief

Objective • Student teachers should be able to plan, organize and manage differentiated activities for pupils.

Time • 6 to 8 hours for the student teacher to plan, organize, teach and evaluate
   • 2 hours for the mentor to discuss, observe and debrief

Background

Student teachers should now have some grasp of a theoretical model which provides some explanation for the notion of 'difficulty', and thereby progression. There are two traps for the unwary: one is over-estimation and the other under-estimation of pupils' capabilities.

The first is to expect pupils to construct high level abstract models such as density, digestion, or chemical bonding from one or two practical activities and sets of observations. Even with able pupils this is unrealistic since the development of such abstract models requires considerable discussion and testing, by the learners, of their ideas in a variety of contexts.

The second trap is to pitch the whole lesson at the level of early or mid-concrete operations: providing, for instance, step-by-step instructions for a practical with no call on explanations for observations; comprehension exercises which simply require the transliteration of certain terms or phrases; or cut-out-and-paste activities where a clear pattern is given to be followed. This is the more insidious trap, since pupils rapidly let you know when you are making unreasonable demands on their ability, whereas it is easy for teacher and pupils to enter into an unspoken conspiracy in which teacher makes no great demands, and pupils are quietly engaged in busy-work which has very little educational value.

Instructions

   • Direct the student teacher to the activity.
   • Discuss the student teacher's plans.
   • Team-teach the planned lessons.
   • Debrief the student teacher after the lesson and set targets for future work.

Discussion points

   • A distinction needs to be made between giving faster pupils more of the same sort of work (which is not very motivating) and giving them more challenging work.

- One approach is to have a common core starting point followed by two sorts of extra work. You could discuss other models that you have tried, but remember to distinguish between models which provide extra work for faster pupils, and models which provide work with different levels of demand for pupils at different stages of development of their thinking capabilities.

9.5 Differentiation

Student Teacher's Brief

Objective

You should be able to plan, organize and manage differentiated activities for pupils.

Instructions

- Choose a topic which you will be teaching within the next week or two. It will probably be best to use Year 9 or 10 if the classes are mixed ability.
- Use the figure below to help you to visualize different activities for pupils, at different stages of progression, in terms of different activities and actions.

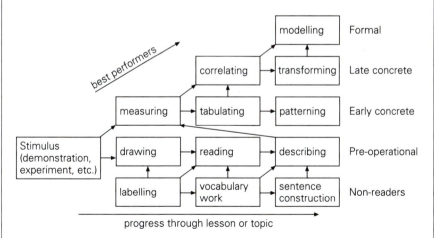

Figure 9.2: One possible way of organizing differentiation of design

- Within the topic you plan to teach, identify a set of objectives which make a range of levels of cognitive demand from early concrete to formal operational.

- Now outline how you would arrange the learning activities so that pupils of different ability could all attain the highest level objective of which they were capable.
  (Possible approaches include providing different worksheets for different pupils; having extra worksheets on hand for those who cope easily with the lower level objectives; and arranging the activity so that less able pupils, who are generally slower, have enough to do at the concrete level while the more able quickly attain the concrete objectives and find themselves with more demanding work.)
- Discuss your plans with your mentor.
- Team-teach the lesson using the differentiated activities for extension work.
- Evaluate the success of the task and plan for future similar activities.
- Discuss your evaluation with your mentor.

Chapter 10

Assessment

Aims

Assessment is a big issue in both the daily life of the school and the way schools and schooling are perceived by the outside world. With such a big topic it has been necessary to be very selective with what has been included here. Choices of activity have been made so that student teachers can begin to operate effectively within the constraints of the system, and with some purpose to their choice of pupil activities. The aims of the chapter are therefore to help student teachers to:

- operate the procedures within the assessment systems of the school
- focus their work within the parameters that are set by school policies on assessment
- gain experience, knowledge and skills in assessment
- reflect on the effective use of information obtained from assessment.

Introduction

In this chapter, assessment means any method, whether formal or informal, for obtaining information about pupil performance. The emphasis is on assessing performance in science. There is no attempt to deal with cross-curricular assessment, the assessment of generic skills and abilities, and the assessment of attitudes and general ability. These are important but are beyond what a newly-qualified teacher needs to know.

This chapter rests upon three basic reasons, of varying locations, for assessment.

- Internally in the classroom: it is impossible to teach effectively without knowing what pupils know, understand and can do.
- Externally in the community: employers and others make use of the results of assessment, and so teachers have a duty to ensure that their pupils do as well they can in these assessments.

- Within the school: school systems require that pupils be assessed for internal record keeping, remedial action, differentiation and progression.

These three reasons encompass the four main purposes of assessment which are given in the report of the Task Group on Assessment and Testing; that is, formative, diagnostic, summative and evaluative. This chapter embraces the first three of these by dealing with four main areas of work in assessment:

- Factual issues — the procedures which have to be followed, either statutorily or by local decision.
- Methods of assessment — the ways of getting information about pupil attainment.
- Pupil involvement — assessment to help pupils to learn.
- The theory of assessment — how do we ensure assessment is valid and reliable?

The theory of assessment, mainly some simple issues of validity and reliability, are integrated into the work of the first three areas. Whilst in practice all the areas interact with each other, for simplicity and manageability they are dealt with separately here.

The main rationale for the order in which student teacher activities are presented is that of student need. It is felt that students will need to know the procedures they have to follow before developing a repertoire of methods of assessment and of the ways to involve pupils. The initial concerns are mainly factual and deal with local and national rules, regulations and procedures for assessing pupils. They cover the framework in which teachers operate. The on-going assessment of pupils is a part of normal teaching. They belong together in practice but are separated out for convenience of coverage in mentoring. Planning assessment should always take place with a clear idea of how the information which is needed will be obtained and how it will be used.

Activity 10.1 introduces homework, marking and record keeping as procedural issues within the school's assessment system. Activity 10.2 turns to external examinations which permeate the classroom through continual assessment and modular tests. The so called 'backwash effect', down from the examinations of Year 11 to more junior years, is important in shaping classroom practice. The planning of teacher assessment of knowledge and cognitive skills is the focus for activity 10.3.

Perhaps the most effective learners are those who are self-aware, for they know where they are going and how far they have yet to travel. Teachers can help pupils become more self-aware of their progress in learning. A simple technique is to organize activities where pupils share their expectations of the questions they might be asked in an assessment. Activity 10.4 is intended to provide student teachers with the opportunity to experiment with such techniques. What is true of pupils is also true for teachers. Student teachers who are self-aware can improve their teaching. Assessment data can be used to provide student teachers with feedback on their teaching, and this is the intention of activity 10.5.

Assessing investigations is a part of the on-going assessment of pupils. It has given rise to considerable concern on the part of teachers. Many of the issues arise out of adopting particular viewpoints on planning, organizing and managing investigations. Therefore this work is to be found in Chapter 5 on investigations. It is a more useful location in this book because it enables student teachers to deal with investigations in one sweep.

Question and answer routines which form the chief activity for assessing pupils' progress ephemerally, and for providing pupils with feedback, are dealt with in Chapter 6.

10.1 Homework/marking/recording

Mentor's Brief

Objectives	• To ensure that student teachers know the procedures for assessing pupils in the school as part of normal teaching activities.
	• To familiarize student teachers with school and departmental documentation.
Time	• 2 to 3 hours for student teachers reading documents and noting points
	• 1 hour discussion with mentor

Instructions

• Collect together the following documents to hand to the student teacher:

> staff handbook and departmental handbook
> school and department assessment policies
> copies of any relevant documentation which is given to parents
> and/or pupils, e.g., homework notebooks and timetables
> examples of work done by pupils which has been marked
> examples of a teacher's record book
> a copy of the department's scheme of work
> a copy of Science in the National Curriculum
> copies of end-of-unit tests and associated mark schemes
> copies of the student materials in this activity

- The student teacher's activity briefs indicate information he or she should extract from the documents. This might be best done as four separate sweeps for the information required in 10.1a, b, c and d separately.
  Familiarity with the documents can be increased in this way.
- Discuss with the student teacher his or her findings and questions.

Discussion points

When discussing the answers to the questions the following should be made clear:

- What the school policy and procedures are
- What the departmental policy and procedures are
- Where the student has choice of action.

10.1a Homework

Student Teacher's Brief

The aim of this activity is to help you find out what the school's homework procedures are within its assessment system.

Instructions

- Collect the materials for this activity from your mentor.
- Make a first search through the documents to find out as much as you can about the following:
  the timetables for setting and handing in homework
  the time pupils are expected to spend on homework
  any special arrangements that exist, e.g., homework clubs
  homework notebooks in which pupils record what they have to do
  the involvement of parents, e.g., signing, or making comments in, the notebook
  procedures for late or none handing in of homework
  the handling of parental complaints, e.g., not enough or too much homework
- Write down things that puzzle you or you are not clear about.
- Discuss these points with your mentor.

10.1b   Marking Books

Student Teacher's Brief

The aim of this activity is for you to familiarize yourself with the school's marking procedures.

Instructions

- Make a second pass through the documents given to you to find out as much as you can about the following:

    are 'rough' books and 'best' books used by the pupils?

    do pupils use textbooks? Do pupils have one of their own?

    can pupils take a book home?

    what is the departmental and/or school policy about marks, grades, levels, etc.?

    try to see examples of marking done by other teachers.

    what is the frequency of marking?

    what are the arrangements for collecting and handing back work done by pupils?

    what feedback should be given to pupils? What should you do about unsatisfactory work, copying, etc.?

- Talk to teachers in other subjects as well as in science about what they do.
- Note down any questions and uncertainties you have.
- Discuss these points with your mentor.

10.1c   Recording

Student Teacher's Brief

The aim of this activity is to familiarize yourself with the departmental record-keeping procedures and systems.

Instructions

- From the materials given to you search through them for a third time to find out the following:

    how is a teachers' record book used?

what use is made of portfolios and other methods of retaining samples of work? This links with activity 10.2 which deals with the key stage 3 tests and the GCSE.

does the school use a system of profiles and/or records of achievement?

how does this operate? The amount of work done on this will depend on the emphasis which the school gives to these.

- Note down points that need clarification.
- Discuss your points with your mentor.

10.1d End-of-unit Tests

Student Teacher's Brief

In this activity the aim is to find out the procedures for dealing with marks that are compiled from end-of-unit tests.

Instructions

- Search the documents for the last time to find answers to the following:

    what are the general arrangements for these tests?
    (End of unit tests are distinguished from GCSE end-of-module tests if the school is following a modular syllabus.)
    where are the tests and marking schemes stored?
    what is the system for gaining access to them?
    how are the results used, for example to provide feedback to pupils or to be stored for Key Stage 3 summative purposes?
- Note down things that puzzle you.
- Discuss the points you don't understand with your mentor.

10.2 External Examinations

Mentor's Brief

Objective • To ensure the student teacher knows the procedures for assessing pupils at the end of Key Stage 3 and Key Stage 4 and is familiar with any other formal assessments, such as A-level and GNVQ, which may take place in the school.

Time
- 2 to 3 hours for student teachers reading documents and noting points
- 1 hour discussion with mentor

Background

Where external examinations are concerned, the requirements of student teachers will depend on what classes they are teaching. While only some schools are involved with GNVQs and/or A-levels and AS-levels, all secondary schools are involved in statutory assessments for Key Stages 3 and 4. For this reason this activity concentrates on the Key Stage 3 tests and the GCSE, however the issues covered should be extended to any other formal examinations with which the school may be involved.

Both the Key Stage 3 assessment arrangements and the GCSE involve a formal written examination and teacher assessment of pupils. This activity concentrates on the procedures which have to be followed in relation to both of these.

Instructions

- Collect together the following documents for the student teacher to review:
  copies of relevant statutory instruments, circulars and the latest information about the Key Stage 3 tests
  examples of previous Key Stage 3 tests
  copies of the regulations and syllabus(es) for the GCSE Board(s) used by the school
  copies of past examination papers
  a copy of the department's scheme of work
  a copy of Science in the National Curriculum.

A good way of covering the procedures which have to be followed for the external examinations is by discussion with the head of department. While there are similarities between the procedures for Key Stage 3 and Key Stage 4, the differences are such that it might be best to deal with the two key stages separately.

The students should have access to all the materials mentioned above and should have their own copies of the department's scheme of work and Science in the National Curriculum. Before any discussion takes place it is helpful for the students to be familiar with the contents of the above materials. To guide them in their reading they can be given the list of issues which will be discussed under the two headings shown below.

Discussion points

Discussion and clarification of the above issues are important. At the same time the structure of science in the National Curriculum should be made clear and related to the scheme of work of the department, particularly if this has not been done elsewhere. As discussion takes place it is inevitable that other important matters will emerge such as the reasons behind the choice of a particular GCSE syllabus, the teaching of 'integrated' science or of separate-subject science.

10.2a Key Stage 3

Student Teacher's Brief

The assessment arrangements for Key Stage 3 are governed by Statutory Orders which are issued each year. The arrangements may, therefore, change from one year to the next.

The following are currently the main issues which should be clarified.

Instructions

- Read the documents you have been given and find out as much as you can about the following:
    the arrangements for writing and issuing test papers and mark schemes
    the arrangement of the written papers
    decisions about entering pupils for the most appropriate tier(s)
    arrangements for pupils with special needs
    absence from some or all of the tests
    marking and recording
    teacher assessment needed in all attainment targets
    the methods of doing teacher assessment are decided by the school
    arrangements for arriving at common standards
    making decisions about a final level
    separate reporting of teacher assessment and test results
- Again note down things that do not make sense to you.
- Discuss your points with your mentor.

10.2b   Key Stage 4 (GCSE)

Student Teacher's Brief

The GCSE is the means of assessing pupil performance at the end of key stage 4, and the detailed arrangements are determined by the relevant Examination Board. Some of the issues are the same as for key stage 3. The major differences are as follows and should be discussed.

- There can be a single subject, a double subject or Biology, Chemistry and Physics taken together. The relevant syllabuses are issued by the Board, and the school will have made decisions about what is available to the pupils.
- Examination papers are marked by an external examiner.
- Teacher assessment is needed only in Attainment Target 1.
- The Board will have issued guidelines for doing teacher assessment.
- The Board will have made arrangements for arriving at common standards.

Through this activity you should become more familiar with GCSE procedures.

Instructions

- Read the documents you have been given and find out as much as you can about the following:
    syllabuses which are available
    writing and marking of examination papers
    what teacher assessment is needed
    guidelines for doing teacher assessment
    arrangements for arriving at common standards.
- Write down points that need clarification.
- Discuss these points with your mentor.

10.3   Teacher Assessment of Knowledge and Understanding

Mentor's Brief

Objectives • Student teachers' should be able to plan the assessment of pupils in relation to their knowledge and understanding of science.

- Student teachers' should be able to carry out the assessment of pupils in relation to their knowledge and understanding of science.

Time
- The activity extends over several weeks and forms a major part of the teaching and observation activities of the student
- ¹⁄₄ hour discussions with the mentor on assessment proposals and evaluations throughout teaching practice

Background

Student teachers will need to know how the on-going assessment of pupils can be used to help pupils progress (formative purposes), and also how the assessment contributes to the decisions made about the pupils at the end of each key stage (summative purposes). This will involve knowing what information is needed and how it can best be obtained.

The student teacher should plan one or more lessons taking particular care to identify the learning outcomes expected of the pupils and to make clear how the achievement of these outcomes will be checked (see Chapter 4 also). A good way to start this is to be involved in the planning of a lesson which will be taught by another teacher, and then to observe the lesson or do some team-teaching concentrating on the assessment opportunities and the information obtained from the assessments. As confidence and expertise grow, student teachers can plan for assessment in their own lessons.

One format for a plan is given in the student's sheet, others are given in *Teacher Assessment in Practice* (SEAC, 1992). Any system which enables the student to concentrate on ways of getting specific information about pupil attainment can be used.

Instructions

- Collect the following documents to hand to the student teacher:
    a copy of the department's scheme of work
    a copy of the National Curriculum in Science
    a copy of *Teacher Assessment in Practice* (SEAC, 1992)
    copies of end-of-unit tests and associated mark schemes
    copies of the student materials in this activity
- Direct the student teacher to read the student teacher activity.
- Discuss the student teacher's planned assessment.
- Review the use of the assessment with the student teacher.
- It is unlikely that any one lesson will provide opportunities to use a wide range of assessment methods, and so this planning exercise should be repeated with other lessons which offer other opportunities.

Discussion points

There should be opportunities to discuss the planning task with the student teacher. The following are some of the points which should be covered:

- In which Year are the pupils?
- What attainment targets are covered?
- Does the plan indicate that a variety of teaching methods will be used?
- What range of levels is being covered? Is the range appropriate for the pupils?
    Level 4 – average 11-year-old
    Level 5 – average 13-year-old
    Level 6 – average 15-year-old
  A common mistake is to try to cover too wide a range of levels in one lesson.
- What image of investigations is in mind?
  Are the SoAs covered as part of an investigation or are they being covered in a 'piecemeal' way?
- Is it clear how the assessments will be made?
- Will the assessments get information about individuals (e.g., by marking the work of individuals) or about the class as a whole (e.g., by whole-class questioning)?
- Is the proposed method of assessment (column 3) appropriate for getting the information in column 2? (This is about validity)
- Should teachers do a lesson-planning sheet for each of their lessons? Where does the balance lie between good preparation and heart failure through over-work?
- Is this planning sheet more useful for planning assessment into a topic rather than into a single lesson? (A topic plan is likely to be more permanent and capable of being given to other teachers as a part of the department's scheme of work. However, it is probably unrealistic at this stage to expect a student to plan a whole topic).

10.3a Planning Teacher Assessment of Knowledge and Understanding

Student Teacher' Brief

During the course of this activity you should plan several assessments for lessons taking particular care to identify the learning outcomes expected of the pupils and to make clear how the achievement of these outcomes will be checked.

Instructions

- Read the 'Notes on forms of evidence' below.
- Draw up assessment sheets similar to the one below for lessons which you will be teaching.
- Discuss your assessment plans with your mentor.

Notes on forms of evidence

Collection of permanent information

Information obtained from class tests is a good source of permanent information which, if not careful, can become the only source. The normal classwork and homework done by pupils gives good additional information which should not be ignored. For this reason, opportunities should be provided for pupils to work on their own, e.g., writing their own notes; their own answers to questions; their own explanations; even though they may have been working in groups. It is necessary to make clear to pupils what 'the rules of the game are'. 'You have been working in groups for the past 20 minutes. Now I want you each to write down in your books your own conclusions from the discussions. I will give you five minutes and there is to be no talking in this time.'

Recording of ephemeral information

This is a matter of having clearly in mind some of the learning outcomes which are planned for the lesson and which might be revealed by the actions of the pupils and by the discussions which take place with each other and with the teacher. Of particular interest are aspects of safety, reading instruments accurately, contributions made by individuals, and the understanding of individuals about what is happening – activities which do not easily give rise to a permanent record and so have to be seen at the time.

Good lesson planning is necessary so that there is an opportunity for you to observe and talk to individuals and then to make occasional notes in your record book and also to write comments on pupils' books. It will not be possible to do this for all pupils in the course of one lesson, but over a period of time which involves several lessons most pupils can be covered.

It is often sensible to concentrate on pupils who have difficulty in writing down their ideas, and also to look particularly at pupils about whom there is a lack of information for one reason or another, e.g., absence, personal problems, disruptive behaviour, not talked to by the teacher for some time. Decisions about which pupils will be looked at should be made while planning the lesson.

Below is an example of a planning sheet for assessment in a lesson.

The main purpose is to ensure that the methods of assessment in column 3 are suitable for checking the proposed learning outcomes for the lesson given in column 2.

Topic   Acids and alkalis
Lesson   Establishing the meaning of pH

Table 10.1:   An example of a planning sheet for assessment in lessons

Activities	Learning outcomes	Methods of assessment
Under this heading, set out the activities which the pupils will be doing. For example: • Class discussion of the meaning of acidity. • Individual reading and making notes about pH. • Individual writing of answers to some questions about pH values. • In pairs writing down the plan of an experiment to determine the pH of different materials.	In this column, give a list of what it is the pupils are expected to learn. Some, but not necessarily all, of the outcomes should relate to statements of attainment in the National Curriculum.	Details of the ways in which information will be obtained about pupils' attainment of the expected learning outcomes should be given. For example: • Talk to a few selected individuals as they are making their notes about pH. Concentrate on those pupils who have difficulty in writing or about whom some specific information is needed. • Collect in books at the end of the lesson and mark the notes and the answers to the questions.

Any system which enables you to concentrate on ways of getting specific information about pupil attainment can be used for planning lessons.

It is unlikely that any one lesson will provide opportunities to use a wide range of assessment methods, and so you should do this planning with other lessons which together will offer a variety of opportunities.

10.3b   Carrying out Teacher Assessment of Knowledge and Understanding

Student Teacher's Brief

Instructions

• Teach some or all of a lesson which you have planned in activity 10.3a.

- Check whether the three columns in the planning sheet match. That is, did the activities in column 1 create the required learning outcomes in column 2, and did the methods of assessment set out in column 3 give information about the learning outcomes for individuals and/or for groups of pupils?
- Discuss your evaluation of the assessment you planned with your mentor.

10.4 Using Question Writing as a Technique for Pupils to take Control of their Learning

Mentor's Brief

Objective
- Student teachers should be able to involve pupils in using assessment of learning objectives to guide and motivate their own learning.

Time
- Several lessons for the student teacher
- $\frac{1}{2}$ hour discussion with mentor

Background

Teachers know what they want their pupils to learn. Teachers also know how the pupils will be expected to show what they have learned in assessments. This information should be shared with pupils so that they can take control of their own learning. Pupils have to be helped to disentangle the essential learning outcomes from the methods which are used in the teaching. For example, a word search properly used can help pupils to become familiar with essential vocabulary and to learn important concepts. However, when asked to do some revision, the pupils may look back on the word search activity which is in their exercise books and wonder why they did it and what the messages are. They are unlikely to be given a word search activity in a test, and so in this case the method of teaching is not the same as the method of assessing. Teachers know this, but the pupils do not unless they are told. By extension, student teachers also need to learn this.

Instructions

- Collect the following materials:
  a copy of the department's scheme of work
  a copy of Science in the National Curriculum.
- Help the student to identify the learning outcomes for a lesson which the student will teach.

- Sit in on the lesson, particularly at the end, or do some team-teaching with the student.
- After the lesson discuss what happened.

Discussion points

Try to identify the successes so that they can be repeated. Try to distinguish what did not work because of the inexperience of the pupils from what did not work because of mistakes made in the teaching.

Use the experience of this lesson to help the student write a pupil prompt sheet for a unit of work. This is quite a demanding task which requires striking the right balance between a lot of detail which is difficult for pupils to embrace, and too much generalization which will mean nothing to the pupils. Monitor the use of this prompt sheet by taking part in one or two lessons while the unit is being taught and by discussing progress with the student from time to time.

10.4a   Using Question Writing as a Technique for Pupils in Lessons

Student Teacher's Brief

This activity is designed to help you to help pupils monitor their own performance. The main aim of the activity for pupils is to get them thinking of the kinds of questions they will have to answer when they are assessed. This will help them in their learning.

Instructions

- Choose a lesson which you are going to teach soon.
- Write down the important learning outcomes of the lesson. Alongside each one write down what the pupils will have to do in order to show their learning.
- Put these into a form of words which the pupils will understand. You should have something like the following.

Learning outcomes	**What you have to do**
Understand the meaning of pH	Be able to write down the pH values for acids and for alkalis. Give the colours for different pH values

- Plan the lesson so that you have a few minutes at the start to explain about the learning outcomes, and about 20 minutes at the end to discuss the outcomes with the pupils.

- At the start of the lesson give the information to the pupils, preferably in writing. Tell them this is what the lesson is about and that you will say more about it at the end of the lesson.
- In the last 20 minutes of the lesson do the following:

  give the pupils a question (it can be an oral question) which is about one of the things they have to know or be able to do following the work in this lesson

  allow time for them to think about the question, then give them the answer

  ask the pupils to write their own question about things they have learnt in the lesson

  ask some of the pupils to read out their question and other pupils to give an answer

  comment on the questions and the answers

  tell the pupils this is what they should do when they are revising.
- Discuss the lesson and the use of pupils' questions as a guide to learning with your mentor.

The idea of pupils writing their own questions in order to test their own understanding is likely to be new to the pupils, and is not easy. They will have to be helped, and they need to do it more than once over a long period of time.

10.4a Using Question Writing for Pupils in Modules

Student Teacher's Brief

The same technique of pupils' questions can be extended into a complete unit or module.

The aim of this activity is to give you some experience with this way of working with pupils.

Instructions

- Locate the pupils' objectives, or revision sheet, in the files for the scheme of work for the unit or module and copy it for the pupils.
- Give out the objectives, or revision, sheet at the start of the unit.
- Explain it briefly to the pupils and tell them to keep it safely because you are going to refer to it frequently while the unit is being covered.

- As you teach the unit make use of the prompt sheet in the following ways:

    at the start of a lesson show the pupils what you intend to cover

    at the end of a lesson show the pupils what has been done

    ask the pupils to write their own comments on the sheet.
- Occasionally do the question writing session as described above.
- Talk to individuals about the sheet. Ask them if they can do the things in the 'What you have to do' column.
- At the end of the unit ask the pupils to use the prompt sheet as a revision sheet.
- Use the prompt sheet to write an end-of-unit test.

10.5 Using Assessment Data as Feedback on Teaching

Mentor's Brief

Objective • Student teachers should be able to use assessment data to provide information to guide modification of their classroom teaching and schemes of work.

Time • 4 to 6 hours for the student teacher to sift pupils responses, reflect and write a report
  • 1 hour discussion with mentor

Background

A claim to professionalism can be interpreted as a claim to critical evaluation of one's own work and a serious attempt to achieve, and raise, standards of practice. The data collected on pupils' performance in assessments can be used to raise the standards of our teaching. In a well run department this is carried out systematically and the results shared corporately. Student teachers need induction into their profession by being given the opportunity to act professionally.

Instructions

- Decide upon when it may be useful for the student teacher to carry out this task in their teaching practice.
- Decide upon which unit or module of work should be looked at in this way. Refer to the work on revising a scheme of work in activity 4.5 and combine analysis of pupils' test responses into that activity if you think this best.

- Offer guidance on the analysis where possible.
- Read and discuss the student teacher's report on revisions suggested following their research.

Discussion points

Some teachers might express concern over the mechanization of the revision of schemes of work in this way. This activity does not take away the need for skill, insight, creativity and flair. Without these a scheme of work can be arid and of little help to other teachers and pupils. The deliberate review of pupils answers, not for marking purposes but for research purposes, can be revelatory.

10.5   Using Assessment Data as Feedback on Teaching

Student Teacher's Brief

How much pupils know about the topics you have taught them, and how much they can use their cognitive skills to work within that topic, depends in part upon your skills as a teacher. In assessing the pupils you are in some ways evaluating your teaching. The assessment data on any one pupil contains information on that pupil. The assessment data on the class as a whole contains information about the activities, teaching sequence and scheme of work that you put into effect. This activity is intended to help you review pupils' responses to test items and to reflect on the implications for your choice of activities and scheme of work.

Instructions

- Collect pupils' scripts for an end of unit or module test for a work that you have taught.
- Scan through the pupils' scores on the test items.
  Find the items that were easiest and those that were answered least well.
- Start with the test item that had the lowest facility: was most poorly attempted.
  Refer to the objectives of the scheme of work to refresh your memory on what the pupils should have achieved.
- Decide if the test item matches the learning objectives in the scheme of work or not.
  If it does not then the test item will need replacement.
- If the test item does match the learning objectives, then decide if the test item had low facility because pupils misunderstood it or not.

If it has been misunderstood then it will need rewriting.
- If the test item has not been misunderstood, then turn to the pupil activities for that bit of work.

  Decide how the work must be changed for the next group of pupils.

  You might consider doing the following:

  changing the sequencing of activities

  replacing an activity

  modifying the structure of an activity

  re-wording an activity

  modifying the tasks for pupils in the activity

  presenting the information in the task using a different mode: graphical, textual, pictorial, diagrammatic, etc.
- Repeat this with test items of the next lowest facility until you feel you have covered as much as is sensible.
- Write up your proposed amendments to the scheme of work.
- Discuss your write-up with your mentor.

Chapter 11

Progress and Potential

Aim

This chapter aims to provide a framework for working with student teachers as they progress through their time with you.

Introduction

The chapter contains student activities and background reading for mentors and is designed to be used following this timetable:

At the beginning of the student teacher's time in school:
11.1a   Getting to know each other
11.1b   Needs and wants
11.1c   Facing problems

After the student teacher has been in school for several days:
11.2a   Targets and goals
11.2b   Assessing starting positions

After the student teacher has taught a few lessons:
11.3   What progress have I made?

After the student teacher has taught for a few weeks:
11.4   Mid-term review

At the end of the student's teaching practice:
11.5   Final thoughts

The first cluster of activities is designed to provide an opportunity to induct student teachers into the department. Each department has its own way of doing this and you may already have standard procedures. It may be that the 'Getting to know each other' activity is done informally at a local pub rather than as a formal activity in school. However, the quicker that the relationship between you and the student teacher is established the better.

The student teacher's institution will run its own assessment system and should train you in how it works. Activities in 11.2a, 11.2b, 11.3 and 11.4 are designed to complement whichever system that you have adopted and not to replace it. The activities focus on the DFEs list of competences (Appendix 1) which were published in their Circular 9/92. These provide a framework for assessing progress in learning to teach but they do give a restricted view of what it is to be a teacher and should be treated as such.

11.1a Getting to Know Each Other

Mentor's Brief

Aim • To find out more about each other so that you can build the relationship between you and the student teacher and so that you can begin to respect each other's experiences and perceptions.

Time • 45 minutes discussion with mentor

Background

We realize that individual departments may well have established strategies for making the student teacher feel one of the department. You may already know something about the student teacher from their training institution. The key point in this activity is to ensure that both you and the student teacher have an opportunity to talk with each other, at some length, somewhere relatively quiet and unhurried. Often snatched conversations during break do not lead to the effective formation of a good relationship.

Instructions

• Start by asking the student teacher these questions (amend this list as you think appropriate):
 When did you decide that you wanted to be a teacher?
 What influenced you to be a teacher?
 What do you expect to gain from teaching?
 What do you think the positive points of teaching are?
 What do you think are the biggest challenges that teachers face?
 What are your biggest concerns about teaching?
 What would you like to be doing in a few years time?
 What kind of teacher do you want to be?
 Imagine yourself teaching in a few months time — if I walk into the room, what will I see? What will you be doing? What type of 'atmosphere' will you be trying to create?

11.1a Getting to Know Each Other

Student Teacher's Brief

The relationship between you and your mentor is critical to your progress. The aim of this activity is to provide an opportunity for you and your mentor to find out more about each other so that you can begin to build that relationship and so that you can begin to realize each other's experiences and perceptions.

Instructions

- Your mentor is going to ask you a series of questions about your previous experiences of education and about your ideas.
- You are going to ask your mentor the same questions at some point during the session.
- Make a note of the questions on paper.

11.1b Needs and Wants

Mentor's Brief

Objective • Student teachers should know the essential basic information about the science department.

Time • 1 hour for the activity
       • ½ hour discussion with mentor

Background

It is assumed that the student teacher has had a general briefing about the school and that they have had an opportunity to read any briefing notes, department and school handbooks.

Instructions

- Although it is assumed that the student teacher has read any documentation provided, you may wish to have copies of the following to hand:
       school prospectus
       school/staff handbook and/or policy statements

departmental handbook
schemes of work
examination syllabuses
safety information (COSHH forms, Hazcards, etc.).

- Explain to the student teachers that the purpose of the activity is to help them to become more familiar with science in the school as part of the settling in process. After listing and grouping their immediate needs and wants (e.g., questions about the department, questions about the school), the student teachers should rank the questions in order of importance (1 = most important), within each group. At a pre-arranged time, you should go through their questions and provide either the answers or indicate where the answers can be found.
- It is impossible to list all the things that students should know at the beginning of their teaching practice but the following examples may help to structure your discussion with the student.

People:
What do I call people?
Who is in the department?
What responsibilities do members of the department have?

Policy:
What discipline procedures exist in the department?
What homework must I set?

Procedures:
Who do I ask about doctor's appointments?
Where do I get photocopying done?
Can I get a key for the laboratories?

Discussion points

Have the student teachers asked questions that they should know the answers to already (through reading documentation already given to them)? If so, find out if they haven't read the material or if the material is unclear. The student teachers should have a permanent record of the points made during this activity for future reference and should be referred to that record as and when necessary.

11.1b Needs and Wants

Student Teacher's Brief

You are a newcomer: you have entered the school knowing little about the people, the place or the policies. You have some immediate needs and there are some things that you want to do or to find out.

Objective

You should know the essential basic information about the science department.

Instructions

- List on paper your immediate needs and wants.
- Put the questions into groups depending on their content (e.g., questions about the department; questions about the school).
- Rank the questions in order of importance (1 = most important) within each group.
- Your mentor will now go through the questions with you and provide either the answers or indicate where the answers can be found.

11.1c   Facing Problems

Mentor's Brief

Objective   • Student teachers should discuss possible problems and agree ways to preempt them.

Time   • ¹/₂ hour for the student teacher
   • ¹/₂ hour discussion with mentor

Background

The student teachers should have seen a few lessons so that they are in a better position to imagine themselves as teachers. They should have read the appropriate school and department guides.

The assumption made in this chapter is that teaching is problematic and that, as a result, training to be a teacher is problematic too. This is a reasonable proposition given student teachers' comments about teaching practice. However, the majority of the problems involved are foreseeable and soluble. This activity focuses on the possible problems that student teachers may face through their own actions, through the actions of others or through a combination of both and on possible strategies for dealing with them.

Instructions

- Explain to the student teachers that the aim of this activity is to raise their awareness of possible problems that they may encounter so as to agree ways in which the problems can be preempted. After having had time to write down as many possible problems that they think that they may experience, they then group their problems and prioritize them. Your task then is to go through the lists discussing the points and helping the student teachers to come up with realistic ways to preempt the problems.

• The most common problems that mentors and student teachers report can be grouped as follows:

Before/after lessons:
> Ordering apparatus — not ordering in advance.
> Planning — inappropriate or unrealistic plans, insufficient differentiation, unrealistic timing.
> Marking/assessment — infrequent, incorrect, unhelpful, too long in being given back.

During lessons:
> Class management — No time warnings, apparatus not distributed adequately, apparatus missing at the end of the lesson, pupils not organized adequately.
> Safety — warnings not given, dangerous situations not noticed or averted.
> Attitude towards pupils — too timid, too aggressive, unfair.
> Delivery — too high, too low, confusing, too fast, too slow.
> Presentation skills — writing unclear, poor use of colour, unfocused OHT.
> Subject matter — incorrect.
> Discipline — too strict, too soft, unfair.
> Lots of activity but not much thinking.
> Lack of variety.
> Questioning — not enough, pupils shouting out not 'hands up', same pupils answering, same type of question.

Not concerned with lessons:
> Attitude — towards staff — too timid, 'know all', 'thoughtless'.
> Punctuality.
> Motivation.
> Appearance.

Some problems may occur even though the student teacher has not done anything wrong. They include:
> Other teachers not being helpful — 'too busy', 'rubbishing' student teacher in front of pupils.
> Technicians not being helpful.

Other teachers are poor role models.
Senior management not backing up discipline procedures.
Poor or missing schemes of work.
Inappropriate curriculum (national curriculum/exam board syllabus).

Discussion points

In some ways this is the most important activity in this chapter. Bringing your experience to bear positively can make life easier for you, the student teacher and the pupils. Raising issues now will make it easier to discuss them in the future. Obviously talking about problems is not the same as facing them in the classroom but the purpose of the exercise is to act as an advanced organizer — giving them a map of the minefield. The student teachers should feel that they have a clearer awareness of the most likely problems that may occur and should have an understanding of the strategies that may preempt some of them.

11.1c   Facing Problems

Student Teacher's Brief

Good teachers are able to deal with problems as and when they occur. Better teachers are able to preempt some of those problems by applying their experience or by thinking 'what if?' As a student teacher you will inevitably have problems.

Objective

You should discuss possible problems with your mentor and agree ways to preempt them.

Instructions

- Write down as many possible problems that you think that you may experience during your time in school. You only have 15 minutes for this part of the activity.
- Group the problems in some way (e.g., before, during and after lessons or teachers, technicians, pupils and parents.
- Now, prioritize the problems in each group.
- Can you think of ways to preempt the most significant problems?
- Your mentor will go through the lists discussing the points

---

and helping you to come up with realistic ways to preempt the
problems.

11.2a Targets and Goals

Mentor's Brief

Objective • Student teachers should know what is expected of them during
their time in school and should be able to explain the programme of activities that has been made for them.

Time • 1 hour for the student teacher
• ½ hour discussion with mentor

Background

It is assumed that the student teacher's timetable of classes, both for observation
and teaching, is known at this stage.

Instructions

• Materials needed:
staff handbook and departmental handbook
student teacher's timetable
class lists
schemes of work
Science in the National Curriculum
Circular 9/92 competence list (see Appendix 1).
• Circular 9/92 is a good place to start in terms of a list of some basic
teaching competences. Explain that, during their time in school a
student teacher is expected to demonstrate competencies in teaching
and to become a professional in terms of attitude and behaviour. The
student teacher reads the list of competences and makes notes when
something is not clear. Your role is to clarify the points that the
student teacher finds difficult to understand (based on your experience).

Discussion points

It is important that the student teacher knows what is expected of him or her
by the teachers, the technicians and the pupils. The student teacher should feel
that they know the boundaries within which they can operate and should feel
comfortable working within them.

11.2a   Targets and Goals

Student Teacher's Brief

The Government, acting on the advice of the Council for the Accreditation of Teacher Education (CATE), has laid down criteria (Circular 9/92) for courses of initial teacher training. Although not exhaustive, they give a clear indication of the important skills and knowledge that you will be expected to develop before you can become a qualified teacher. Such a process of development will take place continuously and will have started already. Indeed, your previous experiences, prior to becoming a student teacher will already have contributed to your development. Now that you have begun to get to know your school, your mentor and yourself better, it is appropriate to look in some detail at where you are now.

Objective

You should know what is expected of you during your time in school and you should be able to explain the programme of activities that has been made for you.

Instructions

This exercise has three parts each with a specific aim:

- Part 1 involves looking critically at the competencies to see if their meanings are clear and to see if you can find any limitations that they may present in describing what being a teacher involves.
- Part 2 involves individually writing your own, possibly tentative, assessment of your position with respect to these criteria and any other criteria that you think are helpful. The aim of this part is to help you to see the progress that you have made and to identify areas where you will need to focus in the coming weeks.
- Part 3 involves discussing your own assessment with your mentor. The aim of this part is to give you an indication of your progress as seen by other people and to provide you with concrete suggestions which will help in your development.
- After you have gone through this exercise your mentor will explain the timetable of activities and classes that have been arranged for you so that you can see the opportunities that you will have to develop the competencies that you have discussed.

11.2b   Assessing Starting Positions

Mentor's Brief

Aim   •   This activity is designed to give the student teachers an opportunity to get some feedback early in their time in school about the initial impressions that they have created. By making it an explicit activity it may give you a forum for feeding back comments that other staff and the pupils may have made to you as well as to give you an opportunity to make your own appraisal of the student teachers' initial impact on the school.

Time   •   1 hour for the student teacher
   •   ½ hour discussion with mentor

Background

Being a teacher is not just about the quality of the learning and teaching that goes on in the classroom. Being a professional has wider implications and responsibilities. It is important that you are able to maintain the student teachers' development throughout their time in school. To do this requires regular intervention on your part. The intervention involves you in focusing the student teachers on their progress. As well as utilizing your own ideas during this exercise, you should have collected comments from other staff either formally, or more likely, informally about their initial impressions of the student teacher. You may have also picked up comments from pupils that may be useful in the discussion.

Instructions

   •   Explain to the student teachers that the aim of this activity is to give them an opportunity to get some feedback early in their time in school.
   •   After writing down what impression they have tried to give and what impression they think that they have given in their first few days in school, you should read through what they have written and comment on it. You must be very careful to be as fair, as positive and as helpful as possible. You may wish to make it a reciprocal activity, that is you allow the student teachers to give their impression of you. This must be handled with as much tact as is necessary to make sure that the end result is positive in terms of encouraging the student teachers to improve on what they are doing because they believe that it is necessary not simply because you tell them that it is desirable.

Discussion points

Ideally, the student teachers should feel reassured that they have made a good start to their time in school and should have some positive feedback from you and your colleagues. They should also have clear ideas, on paper, about what they should aim to do next.

Student teachers who have started badly need to counselled wisely. It is better to flag points now than to have to deal with more established problems later. Don't just give problems — give solutions. Common problems include:

- Over-familiarity with pupils
- Not being sensitive to the micropolitics of the department or the school (e.g., sitting in 'someone's' chair in the staffroom can be perceived as insensitivity)
- Being too demanding of busy staff members' time
- 'Knowing everything about education'
- Being over-critical of what they see in the school.

Solutions generally start with an appreciation of the problem. If you can't see the problem, then you don't need to worry about a solution. Most of the problems above require the student teacher shifting the locus of his or her concern from themselves to others, i.e., thinking about other people's needs and wants as well as focusing solely on themselves. How effectively the student teachers can do this depends on his or her personalities and your effectiveness at persuasion.

11.2b   Assessing starting positions

Student Teacher's Brief

This activity will give you an opportunity to get feedback about how you are doing so far in school. You don't always see yourself as others see you and sometimes you may give a completely false impression of yourself without realizing it. However, it can be argued that you are what *other* people think you are.

Instructions

- Write down what impression you have been trying to give during your time in school. Give some examples of what you have been doing to create a positive impression. This should take about 20 minutes.
- Write down anything that you wish you hadn't done or said to a pupil and to members of staff. This should take 10 minutes at most.
- Your mentor will read what you write and will then discuss what you have written.

11.3   What Progress have I Made?

Mentor's Brief

Aim   • At the end of the activity you should both have agreed on the progress that you think has been made and on the improvements that you want to see. The student teacher should be aware of the help that you will give them to assist in making the improvements.

Time   • 1 hour for the student teacher
       • ½ hour discussion with mentor

Background

This activity is an opportunity for you and the student teacher to take stock of the progress that you have both noticed during the first few lessons that you have seen. You will need to have collected together the notes that you (and other staff) may have made about the student teacher's lessons. You will need to have checked with the technicians whether they have had enough notice of apparatus requisitions or whether they have noticed above average breakages or amounts of equipment missing. You will need to have looked at the books that the student teacher has marked and talked to some of the pupils that have been taught by the student teacher.

Instructions

You may find it useful to start with the 9/92 competence list that you may have used in Activity 11.2a. You could go through this list but that may not be an efficient way of proceeding. It may be better if you focus on the broad headings (see page 202) and use the specific competences if you need to expound on points.

It is difficult at this stage to be positive yet realistic. Problems sometimes occur when mentors have not given student teachers adequate indications that there are areas where they have some concerns about the level of performance. It is critical that you point out as clearly and as carefully as you can what improvements you think are necessary and achievable over the next few lessons. In activity 11.1d, you discussed ways of preempting problems — have any of these problems occurred? Has the student teacher responded to the advice offered?

Discussion points

At the end of this activity you should both have a written record of the progress that the students made so far and of the improvements that the students going to try to make. It is important that the students agree to make changes (if necessary) in what they are going to do.

11.3   What Progress have I Made?

Student Teacher's Brief

Now that you have taught a few lessons you should have a clearer idea about how much progress you have made, what you think your strengths are and where you think you need to make improvements. Your perceptions may not be the same as other teachers or indeed your pupils. The purpose of this activity is to give you a chance to stand back and, with your mentor, to focus on your progress.

Instructions

- Collect together all the feedback that you have had on your teaching so far.
- Under the following headings write down the comments that people have made and then add your own comments. You may need to refer to the list of competences that you looked at earlier in the term:
    Subject Knowledge
    Subject Application
    Class Management
    Assessment and Recording of Pupils' Progress
    Further Professional Development.
- You can either write down the answers to the following questions or you can discuss them with your mentor or both:
    What progress have you made?
    What has gone well?
    What would you not do again and why?
    What improvements do you need to make?
    What goals can you realistically attain over the next few weeks?
    If you could change three things, what would they be (and why)?

11.4 Mid-term Review

Mentor's Brief

Aim •   This activity is another opportunity for you and the student teacher to take stock of the progress that you have both noticed half-way through their time in school. At the end of the activity you should both have agreed on the progress that you think has been made and on the improvements that you want to see. The student teacher should be aware of the help that you will give him or her to assist in making the improvements.

Time   •   1 hour for the student
         •   ½ hour discussion with mentor

Background

You will need to have collected together the notes that you (and other staff) may have made about the student teachers' lessons during their teaching experience and any other relevant data (marked books, requisition slips or apparatus orders, copies of reports to parents, etc.).

Instructions

Activity 11.4a involves drawing a profile of how they felt at different points in the time in school. Use this as a way into discussing the relationship between, how one performs, the feedback that one gets and the way that one feels.

Activity 11.4b involves the 9/92 competence list that you may have used in Activity 11.2a. Once the student teacher has had sufficient time to go through the list of competences, you need to discuss their progress and to agree what changes you need to see and what help you are going to give.

Summary

It is critical that you point out as clearly and as carefully as you can what improvements you think must be made. By this time, the student teacher's habits may be resistant to change and it will require you to agree clear plans for action.

At the end of this activity you should both have a written record of the progress that the student teachers have made so far and of the improvements that they will make. It is critical that the student teachers agree to make changes (if necessary) in what they are going to do.

11.4a   Mid-term Review

Student Teacher's Brief

Now that you are half way through your teaching practice, you should have a clear idea about your progress. The purpose of this activity is to

---

sum up your progress and to use that information to decide what actions you are going to take next.

Instructions

- The diagram below shows a simplified version of a student teacher's profile of their teaching practice. The shape of the line represents how they felt at the time and the words sum up the reasons for the highs and lows.

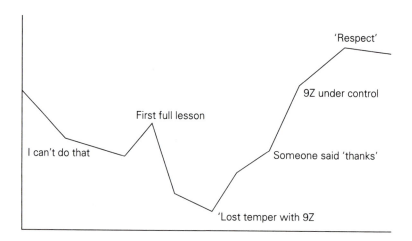

Figure 11.1: *One student teacher's high-point/low-point profile presented at a mid-term review*

- Now, you should draw a more detailed profile for your time in the school. You will use the final profile as a guide to planning the targets for the next part of your teaching practice. Collect together all the feedback that you have had on your teaching so far.

11.4b Assessing your Competence

Student Teacher's Brief

Instructions

- Using the list of competences as a guide, write down what evidence you have about your progress. You will need to discuss what you have written with your mentor.

- You can either write down the answers to the following questions or you can discuss them with your mentor or both:

What progress have you made?

What has gone well?

What would you not do again and why?

What improvements do you need to make?

What goals can you realistically attain over the next few weeks?

If you could change three things, what would they be (and why)?

11.5 Windows of Opportunity

Mentor's Brief

Aims • To provide a the student teacher with a summative assessment of their progress. To provide an opportunity to set targets for the student teacher in terms of future progress.

Time • 1 hour for the student teacher
• ½ hour discussion with mentor

Background

Any formal assessment of the student teacher should have been completed before doing this activity. As one act comes to an end, another is about to begin. Now is a time to look forward to the next steps in the student teachers' career. A time to think of what professional development they will need.

Instructions

- Both you and the student teacher should write down five positive points about their teaching performance.
- You should both also write down five areas for improvement.
- Compare what you have written and then put them into groups as indicated on the activity sheet. Only three of the four 'windows' (A, B and C) will have information in them.
- Your task is to suggest further professional development that the student teachers should consider, both short term and long term. Joining professional organizations, INSET, further degrees, etc. all have something to offer.

Discussion points

Window D represents points that neither of you know about at present. The point to make here is that either another person or a more careful observation on your part or the student teacher's part would be needed to provide something for the fourth window. This involves the student teacher in critical self-reflection or the collection of information from other sources. In Chapter 1 reference was made to teachers as professionals being critically reflective about their own practice. The reflective teacher builds in to their routine work systems to continue professional development.

11.5   Windows of Opportunity

Student Teacher's Brief

By now, you will have had a variety of experiences and you will have learned a lot about teaching and about yourself. Your mentor will have given you feedback about your progress and about your potential. The purpose of this final activity is to share your perceptions about where you are and where you need to go next, in terms of becoming a better teacher.

Instructions

- Write down five positive points about your teaching and five areas for improvement.
- Your mentor will also write down points about your teaching.
- When you have both finished, compare what you have written and put the points into one of the four 'windows' below:

Table 11.1:   A review grid for placing self-analysis and mentor comments for comparison and discussion

	Known by student teacher	Not known by student teacher
Known by Mentor	A	B
Not known by mentor	C	D

The information in Window A is known to you both;
The information in Windows B and C was hidden from one
of you and is now known;
There will not be anything in Window D.

How do you find out what is in Window D?

Critical self-reflection is not automatic and you will need to develop ways of reducing the size of window D. Collecting feedback from pupils in a systematic way is one of the most useful things you can do. For example, monitoring pupils' test results, as in activity 10.5 is a technique you should consider as a routine part of your work.

Appendix 1 — Teacher Competences Reproduced From DfE Circular 9/92

2. COMPETENCES EXPECTED OF NEWLY QUALIFIED TEACHERS

2.1 Higher education institutions, schools and students should focus on the competences of teaching throughout the whole period of initial training. The progressive development of these competences should be monitored regularly during initial training. Their attainment at a level appropriate to newly qualified teachers should be the objective of every student taking a course of initial training.

Subject Knowledge

2.2 Newly qualified teachers should be able to demonstrate:

2.2.1 an understanding of the knowledge, concepts and skills of their specialist subjects and of the place of these subjects in the school curriculum;

2.2.2 knowledge and understanding of the National Curriculum and attainment targets (NCATs) and the programmes of study (PoS) in the subjects they are preparing to teach, together with an understanding of the framework of the statutory requirements;

2.2.3 a breadth and depth of subject knowledge extending beyond PoS and examination syllabuses in school.

Subject Application

2.3 Newly qualified teachers should be able to:

2.3.1 produce coherent lesson plans which take account of NCATs and of the school's curriculum policies;

2.3.2 ensure continuity and progression within and between classes and in subjects;

2.3.3 set appropriately demanding expectations for pupils;

2.3.4   employ a range of teaching strategies appropriate to the age, ability and attainment level of pupils;

2.3.5   present subject content in clear language and in stimulating manner;

2.3.6   contribute to the development of pupils' language and communication skills;

2.3.7   demonstrate ability to select and use appropriate resources, including Information Technology.

Class Management

2.4   Newly qualified teachers should be able to:

2.4.1   decide when teaching the whole class, groups, pairs, or individuals is appropriate for particular learning purposes;

2.4.2   create and maintain a purposeful and orderly environment for the pupils;

2.4.3   devise and use appropriate rewards and sanctions to maintain an effective learning environment;

2.4.4   maintain pupils' interest and motivation.

Assessment and Recording of Pupils' Progress

2.5   Newly qualified teachers should be able to:

2.5.1   identify the current level of attainment of individual pupils using NCATs, statements and attainment and end of key stage statements where applicable;

2.5.2   judge how well each pupil performs against the standard expected of a pupil of that age;

2.5.3   assess and record systematically the progress of individual pupils;

2.5.4   use such assessment in their teaching;

2.5.5   demonstrate that they understand the importance of reporting to pupils on their progress and of marking their work regularly against agreed criteria.

Further Professional Development

2.6   Newly qualified teachers should have acquired in initial training the necessary foundation to develop:

2.6.1   an understanding of the school as an institution and its place within the community;

2.6.2 a working knowledge of their pastoral, contractual, legal and administrative responsibilities as teachers;

2.6.3 an ability to develop effective working relationships with professional colleagues and parents, and to develop their communication skills;

2.6.4 an awareness of individual differences, including social, psychological, developmental and cultural dimensions;

2.6.5 the ability to recognize diversity of talent including that of gifted pupils;

2.6.6 the ability to identify special educational needs or learning difficulties;

2.6.7 a self-critical approach to diagnosing and evaluating pupils' learning, including a recognition of the effects on that learning of teachers' expectations;

2.6.8 a readiness to promote the moral and spiritual well-being of pupils.

Appendix 2 — List of Useful Addresses

The Association for Science Education
College Lane,
Hatfield,
Herts.
AL10 9AA

Tel: 07072–67411

The National SATRO Co-ordinator
Science, Design and Technology Centre,
Middle Lane,
Kingsly, Nr. Frodsham,
Cheshire.
WA6 6TZ

Tel: 0928–788854

British Society for the History of Science
31, High Street.
Stanford in the Vale
Faringdon
Oxon.
SN7 8LH.

Tel: 0367–718963

Note: From 16th April 1995   07072 → 017072
                             0928 → 01928
                             0367 → 01367

References

Chapter 1: Science Teacher Mentoring

CUNNINGHAM, C. and CARLSEN, W. (1994) Expanding the Definition of Subject Matter Knowledge: The Impact of Teachers' Knowledge of the Sociological Nature and Science on their Curriculum Innovations. Paper presented at the American Education Research Association conference, New Orleans, Louisiana, USA, April.

SHULMAN, L.S. (1987) 'Knowledge and teaching: Foundations of the new reform' in *Harvard Educational Review*, **57**, 1, 1–22.

WILLIAMS, A. (1993) 'Teacher perceptions of their needs as mentors in the context of developing school-based initial teacher education' in *British Educational Research Journal*, **19**, 4, 407–20.

Chapter 2: Observing Science Teachers at Work

KELLY, G. (1955) *The Psychology of Personal Constructs. Vols. 1 & 2.* Norton.

National Curriculum Council (1991) *Science: Non-statutory Guidance.*

Chapter 3: Activities for Pupils

BENNETT, N. and CARRÉ, C. (Eds) (1993) *Learning to Teach*. Routledge.

FROST, R. (1994) *The IT in Secondary Science Book: A compendium of ideas for using information technology in science*, IT in Science.

HORTON, P.B. (1992) 'An investigation of the effectiveness of concept mapping as an instructional tool' in *Science Education*, **77** (1), 95–111.

Chapter 5: Science Investigations

SIMON, S.A., JONES, A.T., FAIRBROTHER, R.W., WATSON, J.R. and BLACK, P.J. (1992) *Open Work in Science a Review of Current Practice*, King's College London.

Chapter 6: Communicating Science

BLOOM, B.S. *et al.* (1956) *A Taxonomy of Educational Objectives: Handbook 1: The Cognitive Domain*, Longmans Green.

Chapter 7: Science and Knowledge

FARADAY, M. (1960) *Advice to a Lecturer*, Royal Institution of Great Britain.
NOTT, M. and WELLINGTON, J. (1993) 'Your nature of science profile: an activity for science teachers' in *School Science Review*, **75** (270), 109–112.
WOLPERT, L. (1992) *The Unnatural Nature of Science*, Faber & Faber.

Chapter 8: Science and People

Association for Science Education (1986) *Science and Technology in Society*, ASE.
HEAD, J. (1985) *The Personal Response to Science*, Cambridge University Press.
HODSON, D. (1990) 'A critical look at practical work in school science' in *School Science Review*, **70** (256), 33–40.
KELLINGTON, S. (1982) *Reading About Science. Books 1 to 5*, Heinemann Educational.
WHITFIELD, R. (1979) 'Educational research & science teaching' in *School Science Review*, **60** (212), 411–430.

Chapter 9: Progression in Pupils' Ideas

ADEY, P., SHAYER, M. and YATES, C. (1989) *Thinking Science*, Nelson.
ADEY, P. and SHAYER, M. (1994) *Really Raising Standards*, Routledge.
DRIVER, R. *et al.* (1994) *Making Sense of Secondary Science: Research into Children's Ideas*, Routledge.
SHAYER, M. and ADEY, P. (1981) *Towards a Science of Science Teaching*, Heinemann Educational.

Chapter 10: Assessment

Schools Examinations and Assessment Council (1992) *Teacher Assessment in Practice*, Central Office of Information.

Bibliography

Chapter 1: Science Teacher Mentoring and Chapter 11 Progress and Potential

CLARK, J. (1992) *Management in Education: Vol.2. Managing Others*, Framework Press.

KERRY, T. (1981) *The New Teacher*, DES Teacher Education Project Focus Books, Macmillan Education.

McINTYRE, D., HAGGER, H. and BURN, K. (1994) *The Management of Student Teachers' Learning: A Guide for Professional Tutors in Secondary Schools*, Kogan Page.

SMITH, R. (1990) *The Effective School: Vol. 1. Teachers working together: The Whole School Approach*, Framework Press.

WILKIN, M. and SANKEY, D., *et al.* (1994) *Collaboration and Transistion in Initial Teacher Training*, Kogan Page.

Chapter 2: Observing Science Teachers at Work

CAVENDISH, S., GALTON, M., HARGREAVES, L. and HARLEN, W. (1990) *Observing Activities*, Paul Chapman Publishing Company.

SANDS, M.K. and HULL, R. (1992) *Teaching Science*, Focus on Education Series, Nelson.

Chapter 3: Activities for Pupils

BENTLEY, D. and WATTS, M. (Eds) (1989) *Learning and Teaching in School Science*, Open University Press.

REID, D. and HODSON, D. (1989) *Science for All*, Cassell.

SCAIFE, J. and WELLINGTON, J. (1983) *Information Technology and Science and Technology Education*, Open University Press.

WHITE, R. (1988) *Learning Science*, Basil Blackwell.

WHITE, R. and GUNSTONE, R. (1992) *Probing Understanding*, Falmer Press.

Chapter 4: Planning and Managing

SMITH, R. (1990) *The Effective School: Vol.2. Classroom Techniques and Management*, Framework Press.

Chapter 5: Science Investigations

FAIRBROTHER, R., WATSON, J.R., BLACK, P.J., JONES, A.T. and SIMON, S.A. (1992) *Open Work in Science: INSET for Investigations*, Association for Science Education.

JONES, A.T., SIMON, S.A., BLACK, P.J., FAIRBROTHER, R. and WATSON, J.R. (1992) *Open Work in Science: Development of Investigations in Schools*, Association for Science Education.

QUALTER, A., STRANG, J., SWATTON, P. and TAYLOR, R. (1990) *Exploration: A Way of Learning Science*, Basil Blackwell.

WATSON, J.R., FAIRBROTHER, R., BLACK, P.J., JONES, A.T. and SIMON, S.A. (1992) *Open Work in Science: A Video for Investigations*, Association for Science Education.

WELLINGTON, J. (Ed) (1989) *Skills and Processes in Science Education,* Routledge.

WOOLNOUGH, B. and ALSOP, T. (1985) *Practical Work in Science*, Cambridge University Press.

WOOLNOUGH, B. (Ed) (1991) *Practical Science*, Open University Press.

Chapter 6: Communicating Science

BARLEX, D. and CARRÉ, C. (1985) *Visual Communication in Science*, Cambridge University Press.

BENTLEY, D. and WATTS, M. (1992) *Communicating in School Science*, Falmer Press.

BROWN, G. and HATTON, N. (1981) *Explanations & Explaining*, DES Teacher Education Project Focus Books, Macmillan Education.

BULMAN, L. (1985) *Teaching Language and Study Skills in Secondary Science*, Heinemann Educational.

KERRY, T. (1981) *Effective Questioning*, DES Teacher Education Project Focus Books, Macmillan Education.

SAINSBURY, M. (1992) *Meaning, Communication and Understanding in the Classroom*, Avebury.

SUTTON, C. (1990) *Communicating in the Classroom*, Hodder and Stoughton.

SUTTON, C. (1992) *Words, Science and Learning*, Open University Press.

Chapter 7: Science and Knowledge

DIXON, B. (1989) *The Science of Science: Changing the Way we Think*, Cassell.

DRIVER, R. (1980) *The Pupil as Scientist*, Open University Press.

MATTHEWS, M.R. (1994) *History, Philosophy and Science Teaching*, Routledge.
MEADOWS, J. (1987) *The History of Scientific Discovery*, Cassell.
MILLER, R. (Ed) (1989) *Doing Science*, Falmer Press.

Chapter 8: Science and People

HEAD, J. (1985) *The Personal Response to Science*, Cambridge University Press.
KELLY, A. (1981) *The Missing Half: Girls and Science Education*, Manchester University Press.
KELLY, A. (Ed) (1987) *Science for Girls*, Open University Press.
REISS, M. (1993) *Science Education for a Pluralist Society*, Open University Press.
SOLOMON, J. (1993) *Teaching Science Technology and Society*, Open University Press.
THORP, S. (Ed) (1991) *Race, Equality and Science Teaching*, Association for Science Education.
WELLINGTON, J. (1986) *Controversial Issues in the Curriculum*, Basil Blackwell.

Chapter 9: Progression in Pupils' Ideas

ADEY, P. and SHAYER, M. (1994) *Really Raising Standards*, Routledge.
BELL, P. and KERRY, T. (1981) *Teaching Slow Learners*, DES Teacher Education Project Focus Books, Macmillan Education.
DRIVER, R. *et al.* (1994) *Making Sense of Secondary Science: Research into Children's Ideas*, Routledge.
KERRY, T. (1981) *Bright Pupils in Mixed Ability Classes*, DES Teacher Education Project Focus Books, Macmillan Education.
KERRY, T. and SANDS, M. (1981) *Mixed Ability Teaching in the Early Years of the Secondary School*, DES Teacher Education Project Focus Books, Macmillan Education.
SHAYER, M. and ADEY, P. (1981) *Towards a Science of Science Teaching*, Heinemann Educational.

Chapter 10: Assessment

General
MATHEWS, J.C. (1985) *Examinations*, Allen & Unwin.
ROWNTREE, D. (1977) *Assessing Students: How Shall We Know Them?* Harper & Row.
TUCKMAN, B.W. (1988) *Testing for Teachers* (2 ed.) Harcourt Brace Jovanovich.

Teacher Assessment

FAIRBROTHER, B., BLACK, P. and GILL, P. (Eds) (1993) *Teacher Assessment of Pupils: Active Support*, Centre for Educational Studies, King's College London.

FAIRBROTHER, B., BLACK, P. and GILL, P. (Eds) (1994) *Teachers Assessing Pupils: Studies from Science Classrooms*, Centre for Educational Studies, King's College London.

Profiles

ARCHBALD, D.A. and NEWMANN, F.M. (1992) 'Approaches to assessing academic achievement' in BERLAK, H. (Ed) *Toward a New Science of Educational Testing and Assessment*, (pp.139–180) State University of New York Press.

BALOGH, J. (1982) *Profile Reports for School Leavers*, Schools Council.

HARRISON, A. (1983) *Profile Reporting of Examination Results*, Evans/Methuen.

HITCHCOCK, G. (1986) *Profiles & Profiling: A Practical Introduction*, Macmillan.

Records of Achievement

BROADFOOT, P. (Ed) (1986) *Profiles & Records of Achievement*, Holt, Rinehart & Winston.

BROADFOOT, P. (1992) 'Multilateral Evaluation: A case study of the national evaluation of the records of achievement (PRAISE) project' in *British Educational Research Journal*, 18 (3), 245–260.

BROADFOOT, P., JAMES, M., MCMEEKING, S., NUTTALL, D. and STIERER, B. (1990) 'Records of Achievement: Report of the National Evaluation of Pilot Schemes' in HORTON, T. (Ed) *Assessment Debates*, Hodder & Stoughton/The Open University.

POLE, C.J. (1993) *Assessing & Recording Achievement*, Open University Press.

Statutory Testing Guidance

Schools Examination and Assessment Council (1992a) *Teacher Assessment in Practice*.

Schools Examination and Assessment Council (1992b) *KS3. Science Pupils' Work Assessed*.

Schools Examination and Assessment Council (1993a) *KS3. Science Pupils' Work Assessed: Four Pupils' Folders*.

Schools Examination and Assessment Council (1993b) *KS3. Science Assessing Sc1: Scientific Investigations*.

Schools Examination and Assessment Council (Annually) *End of Key Stage Assessment Arrangements*.

General texts on science teaching and improving performance

BROWN, J. *et al.* (Eds) (1986) *Science in Schools*, Open University Press.

HULL, R. (Ed) (1983) *Science Teachers' Handbook*, Association for Science Education.

LEVINSON, R. (1994) *Teaching Science*, Open University Press.

WELLINGTON, J. (1994) *Secondary Science*, Routledge.

Notes on Contributors

Philip Adey contributed Chapter 10 on Progression. He has extensive research experience in cognitive acceleration and INSET. He was a chemistry teacher, and has authored and edited science textbooks for secondary school pupils from Barbados to Botswana and has been responsible for piloting the new school-based science PGCE at King's College London.

Justin Dillon acted as co-editor. He contributed Chapters 1 and 11. He has taught in several London secondary schools and has research interests in environmental education, information technology in education and school management. He has acted as a consultant to several overseas governments on a variety of different aspects of secondary science education. His current PGCE work involves co-ordinating the part-time PGCE at King's College London.

Bob Fairbrother contributed activities 10.1 to 10.3 on assessment, together with activity 5.5 on 'Raising pupils' performance on investigations'. He has considerable experience in classroom practice, curriculum development, textbook authorship and overseas consultancy. He is a well-known figure for his work within the ASE and his extensive advisory work on assessment.

Christine Harrison contributed Chapter 2 on Observation, with Martin Monk. She is one of the authors of the Bath Science 5-to-16 series at key stages 2, 3 and 4 as well as contributing to other school science text books. She has extensive experience in schools as a teacher, head of department and Inset coordinator. From working as a freelance science education consultant for several years, Chris has recently joined the staff at King's College London, and taken over responsibility for the biology group of students on the PGCE. Her current consultancy work takes her to Nigeria.

Martin Monk acted as the general editor. He wrote Chapters 4 and 7 and contributed to Chapters 2 and 6. His work at King's College London is mostly consultancy for overseas governments and short courses for overseas students. His research interests are focused on knowledge, skills and management.

Jonathan Osborne contributed Chapter 3 on Activities. He contributed Chapter 8, on Science and People, together with Martin Monk. He has co-authored a book on teaching physics for non-physicists which developed out of his experience as a physics teacher with ILEA, as an INSET organizer and physics PGCE tutor at King's. His research interests include alternatives to practical and ways of using different representations of knowledge to help pupils learn science.

Rod Watson contributed Chapter 5, on Investigations. He wrote Chapter 6, on communicating science, with Martin Monk. He has responsibility for the chemistry students on the PGCE at King's College London. His classroom experience in chemical education has led to his collaboration with researchers in countries as diverse as Spain, Malawi and Slovenia. His recent interests and publications have been focused on pupils' investigations in science and progression in children's ideas on chemical issues.

Index